Centralized

Roman Shemakov

Centralized

Notes on Hydraulic and Digital Infrastructure

Roman Shemakov
Beijing, People's Republic of China

ISBN 978-981-96-2936-7   ISBN 978-981-96-2937-4 (eBook)
https://doi.org/10.1007/978-981-96-2937-4

This Palgrave Macmillan imprint is published by the registered company Springer Nature Singapore Pte Ltd.
The registered company address is: 152 Beach Road, #21-01/04 Gateway East, Singapore 189721, Singapore

If disposing of this product, please recycle the paper.

FOREWORD: WHAT IS INFRASTRUCTURE?

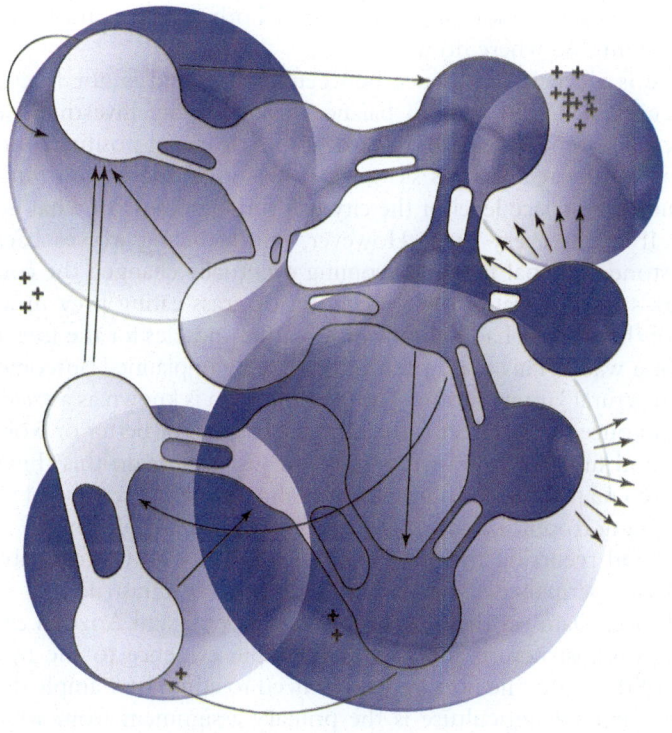

Carbon by Flora Weil

Cities outlast the regimes that build them (and in fact, it is cities that truly build those regimes.) This is the essential power of infrastructure.

Today there is renewed theoretical interest in the politics of infrastructure, but much of the work overlooks the implications of this relationship between builders and the built, between users and the used, between initial and emergent conditions, and between centralization and decentralization. This confusion has implications for understanding the origin of the State, game-theoretical macroeconomics, digital platform theory, not to mention how to effectively redesign the artificial planetary metabolism known as human civilization. Fortunately, Roman Shemakov's book helps set the record straight and points us toward a clearer path.

Among the key plot twists of his story is the imbalance between infrastructural determinism and infrastructures overwhelmed by what they set in motion. Cause causes effect but effect is ultimately its own cause. As a rule, systems set in motion processes that both stabilize and undermine those systems. So where do we start?

There is a crucial difference between what is and is not foreseeable. Infrastructural design tries to balance making a big investment of the resources of time in space toward some clear net-positive outcome. Building a subway system is slow, expensive, loud and boring but in the long run, the surface level of the city will thrive because of what goes on below. It works every time. However, reintroducing wolves back into Yellowstone National Park in Wyoming eventually changed the course of the park's rivers because their predation of grass-eating prey meant the banks of those rivers had radically different boundaries for the free flow of life-giving water. This was a positive but largely unplanned outcome of an "infrastructural" intervention. The phenomenon is known as a *trophic cascade*, and once more, effect is the ultimate cause. For better or worse, the history and future of infrastructure is not just a clear do-this-thing/get-that-outcome policy-driven project; it is also an inexact science of starting and stopping trophic cascades as they spiral in and out of control.

A second recurring theme, one closely linked with determinability, is the relative permanence versus modularity of an infrastructural system. The Hoover Dam on the border between Nevada and Arizona certainly counts as infrastructure and also gives ample evidence to the hydraulic theory of the State, the notion that the need to administer ample distribution of water for agriculture is the primary assignment from which the State apparatus sprung. This Dam thankfully has not changed much since 1935. Very few periodic software patches have altered its flow. Precisely because it is so predictable in performance and reliably inert in form it allowed for the confident investment of human labor and capital to build the urban sprawl of the American Southwest. If the water supply were less taken-for-granted, it's unlikely Los Angeles, Phoenix, or Las Vegas would exist in the way they do today. The stability of the dam makes those crazy unstable cities possible.

However, as the woeful tales of early "Internet" projects makes comically clear, you can't build modular dynamic infrastructures in the same way you build fixed and stable ones. Information is not like water, especially when no one could have foreseen what twists and turns planetary information economies would take. The internet architectures that did work were those that presumed that they could not presume future needs and future technologies, so they built protocol architectures that encouraged the replacement of every component so long as the new component had the same function as the one it replaced. That way, all the other components could reliably send and receive information as usual. It didn't matter if the replaced part in this system was glass or metal, hardware or software. So long as it did what it was supposed to do, the whole apparatus could continuously replace itself, like the Ship of Theseus. You don't want to build a dam that way, but you also don't want to build an internet as a megastructure that will last forever.

The interim takeaway is such: infrastructures with known and stable affordances should be uniquely fixed and unchanging within the ecosystem they give shape to. Infrastructures with unforeseeable and unstable affordances should be designed with prejudice toward modularity and transposition of mechanisms (but not necessarily component functions).

This helps to focus the question at stake. Consider the example (more than a metaphor) of the artificial reef. One predicts that complex ecologies will form, scaffolding from microorganisms up to apex predators, but also that the complexity of that ecology and its energy scaffolds will appear and sustain itself through an ongoing sequence of idiosyncratic instances of energy production and capture, each of which is self-directed.

A common way of evaluating infrastructures is along an imagined spectrum of centralized versus decentralized. Often decentralization is considered both morally and technically preferable because it is apparently more adaptable, dynamic, antifragile, and individualistic. In many cases highly decentralized systems are indeed those things, but even those may not be as decentralized as they appear. The same goes for apparently centralized infrastructures that depend upon both predictable and unpredictable interactions with free-range users. Those relations are so automatic they appear even when not directly intended. Consider artificial ocean reefs as exemplary infrastructures, such as the old battle tanks that the US Army sinks in the ocean. These become the foundation for vibrant little cities of plants and fish. From a wide view, the process is highly predictable. Sink a tank, wait a while, get an ecosystem. This is analogous to laying a power grid, wait a while, get an ecosystem. But the initial act of design only sets things in motion. Unlike a Master Plan, it does not need to manage the details. For the submerged tank, one predicts that complex ecologies will form, a new metabolism is grown, scaffold by scaffold, from microorganisms up to apex predators, but also that the complexity of that ecology and its energy scaffolds will appear and sustain itself through an ongoing geometric sequence of idiosyncratic instances of energy production and capture. Each instance is "determined" both by the local intention of each little actor, some essentially mindless, and also by the available opportunities that accumulate through the ongoing interactions, inputs and outputs. The more interactions the more opportunities and thus more interactions.

Is this centralized or decentralized? It is both, one because of the other. All the organisms emerge from and are drawn to the singular hulking location of the submerged tank. In the empty expanse of the ocean floor this one structure is the place where energy production and circulation is intensely concentrated. In this respect, the infrastructure is centralized. But everyone is free to come and go as they like (imagining that fish have free will). No orders are issued. No forms are filled out. No planning committee decides what happens next. In this sense the architecture of what emerges through and because of the centralized infrastructure is highly decentralized. The centralized initial condition of the iron-rich body of the tank requires the decentralized polyscalar animal-vegetable metabolic economy in order to become an infrastructure *for* something. That decentralized metabolic economy requires the big undemocratic gesture of installing a giant hunk of metal to start the process and to give a rigid shape to its unfolding.

This is not a paradox but in fact the norm. There in fact many possible combinations. The uncertain ratios between fixed and unfixed, initial condition versus emergent condition, are themselves highly contingent, and as Shemakov shows, history is replete with examples of success and failure to align one with the other. One pattern is that infrastructures with fixed and known affordances (provides water) are not only more durable but also more amenable to successful deployment by the dumb unstoppable force of a centralized political agent. However, infrastructures with dynamic and largely unknown affordances (such as the early internet) should be more modular, dynamic, and self-organizing and so when a centralized force-agent tries to implement them, their inclinations to concretize set solutions means they build not vibrant networks but almost immediately obsolete behemoths. The inverse may be true. Highly decentralized forms of political agency are not good at developing and enforcing the installation of big dumb fixed-affordance infrastructures. Anarchist collectives are not good at building intercontinental highways, but the highway gives birth to anarchism. In other words, it takes an army to build and sink a tank, but it takes the chaotic process of accumulating micro innovation to build the life that grows on it.

Artificial intelligence surely is an infrastructure of the future, and unfortunately one of the most widely used comparisons is with the regulation of nuclear power, including the regularly suggested need for an analogous body to the Nuclear Regulatory Commission. However, while it is quite clear what nuclear power does, it is not remotely clear what the ultimate affordances of machine intelligence will be. Regulating it as one would regulate a bomb is to guarantee a trophic cascade of net-negative consequences.

Another interim takeaway: we have in progress a 2 × 2 diagram with our analytical combinations. Projects driven by a centralized state toward a centralized infrastructure, a decentralized state toward a centralized system, a centralized state toward a decentralized system, and a decentralized State toward a decentralized system. Some combinations have better track records than others, but each has its purpose.

As mentioned in Shemakov's first chapter, the formalization of a "hydraulic theory of the State" is attributed to Karl August Wittfogel and his 1957 book with a charming name, *Oriental Despotism: A Comparative Study of Total Power*. Roughly stated, the state evolved in correspondence with the composition of complex integrated technical systems that could not emerge through piecemeal interactions but which required collective foresight, investment, and enforcement. What is called "the State" came to be that which did those things. There is much to accept and also debate about the claim, depending on how expansive one defines all those terms.

What is certain, however, is that in 2025 private corporations have just as much agency to perform State-scale feats of infrastructuralism as any State. They don't have (1) militaries and (2) circumscribed areas on the map, but this is less critical now than historically. This implies many possible futures. Perhaps the *de facto* sovereignties of everyday society are increasingly privatized. Perhaps the agents of *de facto* industrial policy are dispersed about an irregular quilt of transnational hemispherical geopolitics, defined by competition between which great power can build its version of planetary infrastructure faster, and so on. Perhaps both.

As for the renewed focus on the politics of infrastructure, all of this may imply that many are asking the wrong questions. Despite appearances, the real "power" of infrastructure is not in who makes it, who designs it, who commissions it, or who guards it. This is the crucial point: "power" is in how the structure sets things in motion, giving path dependency to these outcomes greater than itself. The power of infrastructure is in how it sparks the combustion of energetic cycles *beyond* the intentions and even the imaginations of its authors.

Consider the urban street grid. It is usually imposed upon a terrain by the singular authority of a planning agency, projecting the most inflexible and rigid geometry of lines and cells imaginable. And yet, it is *because* of the structure provided by this originary imposition that the most vibrant and lavish urban cultures have blossomed. The comparatively whimsical-shaped wandering cul-de-sacs of suburbia may be less regular and standardized, but their effects are not.

Consider as well that infrastructures need not be "big heavy grey things behind a fence" but, like internet protocols, may be rules by which future assemblages must abide in order to ensure compatibility, and the transference of energy, information, and matter. Again, who matters less than what. The metric system not only describes the length and width of objects, but it also more importantly prescribes their sizes. Your 10-cm gizmo and my 10-cm gizmo are thus interoperable and so, thankfully, the costs of building something more valuable and complex with our combined gizmos are radically reduced. Sigh of relief. The material world is democratized because no one has to make every single unique specification. Like organs in a living body, metricized components settled toward standardizations, because of deliberate but arbitrary acts of deliberate artificialization that could never had anticipated what they enabled.

The social relations between any two people are mediated by infrastructures that exceed the scale and scope of anyone's immediate view. In an age of planetary computation, mineral sourcing, supply chains, tech coupling and decoupling, labor arbitrage, computational currencies, water wars, and more, both the formal infrastructures that are built by states and corporations as well as the emergent infrastructures built bottom-up by those solving local problems in ways that become durable systems, "politics" as a whole seems to want to dissolve into infrastructural pre-programming.

Lastly, the politics of infrastructure is defined by the *depoliticization* of the function of the infrastructure. This depoliticization is its success, not its failure. Considering the hydraulic state, it does enormous political agency to build a public water supply. However, once built, turning on a faucet thankfully does not require collective debate among stakeholders to come to a democratic decision as to whether or not you can have water. If the system is what the system does, then the passage from hydropolitics to automation is what the system does.

California, San Diego   Benjamin Bratton

CONTENTS

CHAPTER 1

Canal

Drought by Flora Weil

© The Author(s), under exclusive license to Springer Nature
Singapore Pte Ltd. 2025
R. Shemakov, *Centralized*,
https://doi.org/10.1007/978-981-96-2937-4_1

Abstract This chapter explores the histories of water management and ecological mythmaking in the American Southwest and China. From Jack Swilling's rediscovery of the Hohokam irrigation network that laid the foundation for modern Phoenix, to China's hydraulic engineering legacy rooted in the Yangtze and Yellow Rivers, the chapter describes how water infrastructure has shaped civilizations and driven political power. Linking these regions through the planetary dust cycle, the narrative examines the shared environmental challenges of drought and the global consequences of environmental manipulation.

Keywords Hydraulic engineering • Irrigation • Megadrought • Desertification • Atmospheric rivers • Infrastructure myth

In the 1860s, a restless young adventurer named Jack Swilling spent years in the unforgiving American Southwest engaged in one of the country's favorite pastimes: running from his past and trying to get rich. After years of rough living, he made an unusual discovery that would alter both his life and the destiny of the region.

Scouting through the Salt River Valley, Swilling glimpsed faint markings and mounds of earth that stretched for miles across the arid Arizona landscape. He followed the paths, accidentally discovering the remains of a colossal water transfer system—an advanced irrigation network that rivaled the Roman aqueducts in both scope and engineering precision.

The Hohokam civilization, once the American Southwest's predominant power, had begun meticulously forging this sinuous system of hundreds of miles of waterways across the arid desert as early as the first century CE. With water sourced from the distant Salt River, the Hohokam likely cultivated more than 10,000 acres of arid land. The capillaries of their sprawling water infrastructure allowed the small city-state to tower over neighbors, amassing tributes and military support from surrounding tribes. Engineering and maintenance of this vast agricultural system required a centralized order to flourish for hundreds of years.

Around 1500 the Hohokam disappeared with barely a trace. The exact causes of the collapse remain unsolved, but to the best of modern understanding, it was primarily due to drought that even the expansive irrigation system couldn't manage.

For Swilling, however, the remains of this water infrastructure became an opportunity. He founded the Swilling Irrigation and Canal Company and set out to rebuild the Hohokam canal network. By 1867, water flowed from the Salt River more than 200 miles away to nourish a nascent agricultural industry. The oasis required a fitting name. Among Swilling's ensemble of entrepreneurs and criminals, the Englishman Darrell Duppa proposed the name "Phoenix." According to Duppa, "A great race once dwelt here, and another great race will dwell here in the future. I prophesy that a new city will spring, phoenix-like, from the ruins and ashes of the old."

A century and a half later, the American Southwest is sweltering under another harsh drought, just as Phoenix has become one of America's fastest-growing cities, a trend bolstered by preferential tax schemes and the growth of the (very water-hungry) semiconductor industry. The desert city now has America's largest manufacturing capacity for advanced chips required to power everything from data centers and electric cars to F16s.

But the deep drought across the parched landscape haunts citizens and local politicians alike. The once unthinkable prospect of running out of water has become thinkable in 2023 when 1000-foot wells dug deep underground by residents of Rio Verde, a community on the outskirts of Phoenix, came up dry. The neighboring city of Scottsdale stepped in to help, hauling water to Rio Verde homes in trucks. Then in January of 2023, those too were halted. This has been a familiar sight in drought-stricken regions across Central Asia, Western China, and Sub-Saharan Africa. Today, the unthinkable has finally reached America. One Arizona resident noted, "Hell yes, there's a panic. We're on the front lines of the panic. As it looms and gets closer, of course now more people are opening their eyes going, 'Oh my gosh, this is actually a real thing.'"

The cause—and perhaps solution—of the multi-decade megadrought stifling the American Southwest on a scale not seen in more than a millennium is tied in surprising ways to another desert, one on the other side of the world. Seven thousand miles away, in the Taklamakan Desert, iron-rich dust is blown into the jet stream that links Western China to the Western United States. This sand, scientists have found, contributes to rainfall in America, a reminder of the planetary equilibrium the two countries are intimately enmeshed in.

ECOLOGICAL MYTHMAKING

In both China and the United States, ecological myths have played a key role in shaping national identity. Whether it be the American frontier and the veneration of national resources or China's geological transformations and the quest to control a tumultuous nature, these myths have evolved into a vital source of political legitimacy. In both countries, leaders have imbued nature with religious overtones, rendering it an essential backdrop within the political environment—"Build Back Better" in the United States and "ecological civilization" in the People's Republic.

Chinese legends tell of a time in ancient history when ten suns simultaneously shone on the Yellow River Civilization (黃河文明), leading to an apocalyptic drought followed by a great flood. Yu the Great (大禹), a mythical engineer-king, used clay stolen from the gods to build dikes and dams, quelling the raging river and inaugurating dynastic rule in China that lasted for thousands of years.

For much of Chinese history, emperorship was tightly bound to successful water resource management. Unlike Biblical or Greek mythologies, natural catastrophe was rarely seen as divine retribution for sins, but rather a constant possibility in an anthropic universe that the administrative bureaucracy must perpetually anticipate. The collapse of political order and dynastic transitions have been intimately tied to natural disasters, especially on the Yellow River, throughout China's history.

Starting around 1048 CE, flooding on the Yellow River caused the deaths of over a million people and contributed to the demise of the Northern Song Dynasty. In the 1600s, cataclysmic flooding and the destruction of dikes took the lives of an estimated 300,000 people, striking a critical blow to the already struggling Ming Dynasty. Between 1851 and 1855, massive floods resulted in hundreds of thousands of deaths and led to the Taiping Rebellion, the deadliest civil war in human history. Even today, China's political and economic future remains dependent on the predictable and consistent flow of its two most important water arteries, the Yangtze and the Yellow Rivers.

The concept of "hydraulic despotism," first coined by historian and political theorist Karl August Wittfogel in 1957, is deeply rooted in this historical context. Wittfogel argued that centralized control of water resources served as the foundation for the creation and maintenance of many global empires, particularly in China. The bureaucratic demands of governing thousands of miles of unpredictable rivers and nurturing fragile agriculture necessarily led to centralized administrative control. In fact, water management was so imperative in Chinese society that it dominated all other aspects of life, determining property rights, political power, and economic development. The central thread of this book, both in connection to water and internet management, is this exact premise of institutional determinism—does a bureaucracy create infrastructure or does the infrastructure sustain a bureaucracy?

At the same time as Rio Verde residents were drinking the last drops of their well water, China was sweltering under a stifling drought of its own. A devastating 11-week heatwave pushed the Yangtze, the world's third-longest river and a source of drinking water for 400 million people, to its lowest recorded level. In the eastern Chinese province of Anhui, the government started hauling water by truck to help struggling citizens as well.

In the early 2010s, China and the United States might have worked together to overcome these crippling environmental conditions. The two countries had even announced a collaborative effort to curb emissions and work together on climate solutions as recently as 2013. It was an ambitious agreement between the top two polluters. Yet, such cooperation is less likely today. Global environmental cycles remain jurisdictionally and politically untouchable. Simultaneously, the requests for urgently needed research are all filtered through an economic rivalry, obscuring the reality that both are on a path of environmental destruction bounded by planetary chemistry and a shared infrastructural history.

ARCTIC POLAR VORTEX

The American and the Chinese deserts have been consistently shaped by a history of cyclical droughts, a fact well recorded by the regions' tree rings. But the ongoing megadrought in the American Southwest has been recorded as the worst in 1500 years. Emerging research over the last decade suggests that the source of the prolonged and uncontrollable American drought may be intricately linked to the Taklamakan Desert in Western China's Xinjiang province. Depending on the year, approximately 20 atmospheric rivers—jet streams that bring rain—pass across the U.S. West Coast every year. Together these atmospheric rivers supply more than half of the precipitation that falls across California and the Southwest.

In the early 2010s, researchers compared two atmospheric rivers over the Pacific Ocean that were identical in temperature and water content. One contained dust from the Taklamakan Desert that it had picked up after a sandstorm in Western China and carried across the Pacific. It released almost 40 percent more water than the one without desert dust— a difference of 1.5 million acre-feet of water, more than all of the water in California's largest reservoir.

The Taklamakan Desert—nicknamed the "Place of No Return" in the local folk history—is encircled by mountain ranges: the Kunlun in the South, the Pamir in the West, and the Tian Shan in the North. Over the course of millions of years, winds have shaved these mountains into a reserve of finely ground dust. During a storm, the sand has nowhere to go but northeast, toward the Siberian jet stream. More than 400 million tons of sand from the Taklamakan and other Asian deserts are blown over the Pacific every year.

For atmospheric rivers to drop rain, water particles must coagulate and become heavy enough by icing over. The icing can be accelerated with certain minerals, like the artificial silver iodide used for cloud seeding. In 2013, scientists discovered that a group of minerals called potassium feldspars were natural cloud seeders; their crystal structure offers an extremely convenient scaffolding for water molecules to bind to. While K-feldspars, as they are known, make up a tiny proportion of dust on a global scale, they are abundant in the Taklamakan.

Even more importantly, the Taklamakan dust that ends up in the American West carries "hitchhikers"—desert microbes whose biological structure is designed to survive in the hot desert and also protect them on a winding journey across the Pacific. This dust also carries particular viruses, which (unlike bacteria) are often protected by a solid protein casing, a lattice figure of alternating positive and negative charges that water molecules easily latch onto. Similar winds bring sand from the Sahara to feed the Amazon rainforest and from the Mojave Desert to the Colorado Plateau. Every day, minerals and microorganisms journey across the planet, wafted aloft into the atmosphere among the clouds, maintaining vast and elaborate planetary relationships.

Atmospheric wind connections between the United States and China have shifted considerably in recent decades, and the frequency of dust storms in Northern China has decreased. This is partly due to China's Three-North Shelterbelt initiative that planted millions of acres of forest across Northern China to hold back the deserts. Taklamakan dust is also not as effective in the presence of air pollution, which has increased significantly along the U.S. West Coast and throughout Northern China.

This particular planetary relationship between sand and rain that connects these two deserts began more than 25 million years ago, during the Oligocene Era's tectonic uplift of the Tibetan-Pamir Plateau, which enclosed the area that became the Taklamakan Desert. This geochemistry does not have political borders or allegiances. Simultaneously, our anthropogenic world of international relations is agnostic to these geological epochs, which to its detriment misses something fundamental in the distinction between "geopolitics" and "politics." The drying of cities such as Phoenix and San Diego, for example, is linked to the anti-desertification measures in Kashgar, one of China's westernmost cities. Planting more trees there, paradoxically, could mean less rainfall halfway across the world.

THE GREAT PLANS

If the Taklamakan Desert's most important export to the American West is dust, then the American West's most important export to the Chinese desert is a modern hydrological imagination. The inspiration to control the Yangtze River, which has become the bulwark of the planet's most important economic corridor and a key pillar in China's anti-desertification fight, came from the American Southwest.

In the 1940s, Chiang Kai-shek hired the designer of the Hoover Dam, John L. Savage, to conduct a feasibility study for a similarly ambitious project in China. After a year of carrying out surveys and estimates, Savage returned to the United States and published a proposal for the "Yangtze Gorge and Tributary Project"—or as he called it, "the dream dam."

After the Chinese Communists triumphed over the Nationalists in 1949, Mao Zedong envisioned an elaborate infrastructural scheme to support China's industry and hamper the desert's northward spread by rerouting and damming the Yangtze. In 1956, he wrote a poem that reads in part:

> Great plans are afoot:
> A bridge will fly to span the north and south,
> Turning a deep chasm into a thoroughfare;
> Walls of stone will stand upstream to the west
> To hold back Wushan's clouds and rain
> Till a smooth lake rises in the narrow gorges.
> The mountain goddess if she is still there
> Will marvel at a world so changed.

Mao revived Savage's vision, which, long after they had both passed on, became the Three Gorges Dam and the South-North Water Transfer Project. The former, completed in 2012, is the world's largest hydroelectric dam. The latter, intended to be completed in 2050, will redirect 45 billion cubic meters of the Yangtze via three canals to the north. In 2023, the river diversion's price tag ballooned to $100 billion, making it the most expensive infrastructure project in human history. At the same time, parts of the Yangtze ran completely dry, forcing citizens to rely on water shipments until the rain returned.

The Colorado River, which served as the inspiration for the management of the Yangtze, has reached a similarly critical low point and is struggling to sustain the world it created. Annually, the river provides more than a quarter of the water consumed in Los Angeles, San Diego, and Phoenix. It is essential for most of the country's winter produce; its power illuminates Las Vegas. It is responsible for the boom of the American West, and it may become the bane of its existence.

In his book *Cadillac Desert: The American West and Its Disappearing Water*—a history of the water infrastructure that gave birth to the modern United States—Marc Reisner highlighted this conflicted legacy: "To some conservationists, the Colorado River is the preeminent symbol of everything mankind has done wrong — a harbinger of a squalid and deserved fate. To its preeminent impounder, the U.S. Bureau of Reclamation, it is the perfection of an ideal."

The Colorado River's Hoover Dam was the largest in the world at the time of its construction in 1935: it rose more than 700 feet high and used about 6 million tons of concrete. Normally, it would take 100 years for that amount of concrete to harden. Savage's cooling design—miles and miles of tubes running freezing water through the structure—brought the timeline down to less than two years.

Today, a drought lasting more than two decades could spell disaster for the Colorado River and its 40 million beneficiaries. As Reisner concluded, "one could say that the age of great expectations was inaugurated at Hoover Dam — a 50-year flowering of hopes when all things appeared possible. And one could say that, amid the salt-encrusted sands of the river's dried-up delta, we began to flounder on the Era of Limits."

BIBLIOGRAPHY

Lustgarten, Abrahm. "40 Million People Rely on the Colorado River. It's Drying Up Fast." *ProPublica*, August 27, 2021. https://www.propublica.org/article/40-million-people-rely-on-the-colorado-river-its-drying-up-fast.

Ren, Annie Luman. "The Three Gorges Dam: A Deluge of Doubts." In *The China Story Yearbook 2020: Crisis*. Canberra: Australian Centre on China in the World, 2020. https://www.thechinastory.org/yearbooks/yearbook-2020-crisis/forum-broken-river-shattered-mountain/the-three-gorges-dam-a-deluge-of-doubts/.

Gui, Ke, et al. "Two Mega Sand and Dust Storm Events over Northern China in March 2021: Transport Processes, Historical Ranking and Meteorological Drivers." *Atmospheric Chemistry and Physics*, 2021. https://acp.copernicus.org/preprints/acp-2021-933/acp-2021-933.pdf.

Fox, Douglas. "The Dust Detectives." *High Country News*, December 22, 2014. https://www.hcn.org/issues/46-22/the-dust-detectives/.

Chang, Alvin. "What Tree Rings Reveal about America's Megadrought." *The Guardian*, June 17, 2021. https://www.theguardian.com/us-news/ng-interactive/2021/jun/17/tree-rings-america-megadrought-visual.

Bradsher, Keith, and Joy Dong. "China's Record Drought Is Drying Rivers and Feeding Its Coal Habit." *The New York Times*, August 26, 2022. https://www.nytimes.com/2022/08/26/business/economy/china-drought-economy-climate.html.

Liu, Bin, et al. "Earliest Hydraulic Enterprise in China, 5,100 Years Ago." *Proceedings of the National Academy of Sciences* 114, no. 52 (December 4, 2017). https://doi.org/10.1073/pnas.1710516114.

Storozum, Michael, et al. "The Collapse of the North Song Dynasty and the AD 1048–1128 Yellow River Floods: Geoarchaeological Evidence from Northern Henan Province, China." *The Holocene* 28, no. 11 (August 2, 2018). https://doi.org/10.1177/0959683618788682.

Latzman, Phil. "These Arizona Residents Are in Danger of Being Cut Off from Their Water Supply." *KJZZ*, August 27, 2022. https://www.kjzz.org/2022-08-27/content-1805471-these-arizona-residents-are-danger-being-cut-their-water-supply.

CHAPTER 2

Levee

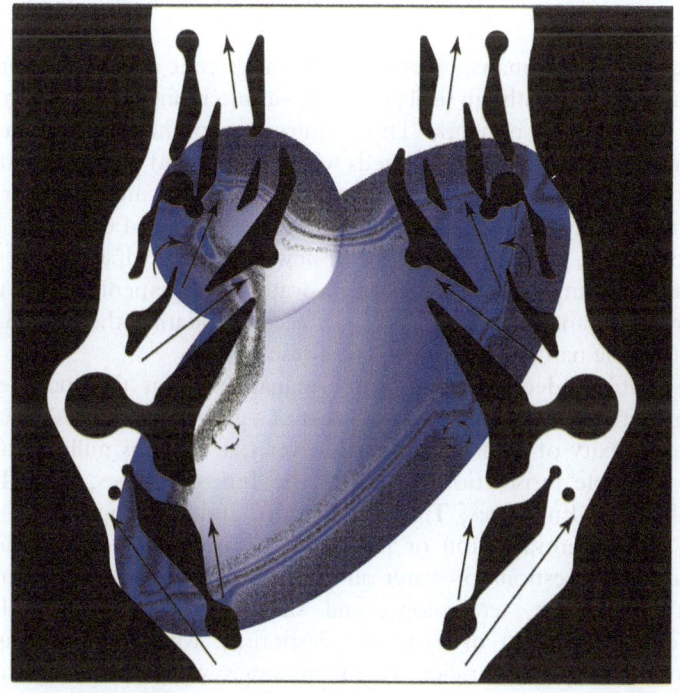

Dujiangyan by Flora Weil

© The Author(s), under exclusive license to Springer Nature
Singapore Pte Ltd. 2025
R. Shemakov, *Centralized*,
https://doi.org/10.1007/978-981-96-2937-4_2

Abstract This chapter examines the tension between centralized and decentralized approaches to water management in the context of historical precedents and modern challenges. Using the Dujiangyan Irrigation System as a case study, it highlights how centralized hydraulic infrastructure transformed regional agriculture, fortified state power, and facilitated China's unification under the Qin Dynasty. The chapter contrasts this success with the Qing Dynasty's eventual collapse in the twentieth century, attributing its failure to fiscal and ideological constraints that deprioritized maintenance of critical water infrastructure.

Keywords Hydraulic statecraft • Qin unification • Qing collapse • Dujiangyan irrigation system • Infrastructure bureaucracy

Centralizing water management demands a systemic approach, approaching water flows—both physical and legal—as interconnected elements of a larger hydrological network. This requires comprehensive and strategic oversight to synchronize local needs with regional and global imperatives, transforming water into a vector of coordination that merges governance with technology. Yet, this centralization raises profound questions about control, access, and the emergence of new forms of hydraulic hegemony. The real challenge is in architecting a water management system that is both resilient and adaptive, capable of accommodating the dynamic and unpredictable nature of water as a vital resource.

By contrast, decentralizing water management at the local level is administratively disastrous in the context of a global water crisis. The intricate complexity of managing a single river that sustains millions of lives across multiple jurisdictions—such as the Indus, Ganges, Amu Darya, Karnali, Nile, Euphrates, Tigris, Colorado, and Mekong Rivers—illustrates that decentralization or jurisdictional subdivision fails to address fundamental questions of water allocation. This is the crucial juncture where governance, technology, and survival intersect, demanding a uniquely modern era of hydraulic despotism. Mitigating the risks of resource scarcity and conflict in an increasingly water-stressed, politically tenuous, and economically precarious world necessitates an integrated approach to governance to ensure viable water usage into the future. Such lessons are not without historical precedent.

The construction and design of the Dujiangyan Irrigation Project, in China's central Sichuan province, traces back over two millennia. At the time of its construction, it represented a remarkable feat of engineering that has left an indelible mark on the socio-political fabric of China. Started under the Qin Dynasty, it consisted of a series of canals, dams, and levees, all meticulously crafted to regulate the flow of the Minjiang River and redirect water for irrigation. The project heralded a profound transformation in agriculture throughout the region, ushering in a new era of productivity that founded a prosperous farming community where it previously did not exist.

DUJIANGYAN AND BIRTH OF CHINA

The Warring States period (475–221 BC) was a political and intellectual crucible of chaos, marked by a relentless struggle among seven states and the hundred schools of thought, each vying for dominance over the landmass now considered China. Amidst this turmoil, the Qin State, initially perceived as a lesser contender, engineered its path to supremacy through strategic innovations in hydraulic infrastructure. Central to this ascension was the construction of the Dujiangyan Irrigation System, a transformative project that stabilized the food supply, supporting military excursions that would ultimately unify China in 221 BC.

Constructed around 256 BC in Sichuan, the Dujiangyan system exemplified the Qin State's mastery of environmental control and resource management. Positioned on the Min River, the longest tributary of the Yangtze, the system addressed both irrigation and flood control. The Min River, descending from the Min Mountains, surged and then abruptly slowed upon reaching the Chengdu Plain, depositing silt and causing devastating floods. Recognizing the strategic importance of mastering this river, King Zhao of Qin commissioned the Dujiangyan project, allocating 100,000 taels of silver and mobilizing tens of thousands of workers. Under the direction of the engineer Li Bing, the project introduced innovative water management methods that emphasized channeling and dividing the river's flow, rather than conventional damming.

The system's centerpiece was a fish-shaped water-diversion levee, constructed from bamboo baskets filled with stones and anchored by wooden tripods. This structure took four years to complete. A formidable challenge was excavating a channel through the mountain, a task that would have taken decades with the hand tools of the era. Li Bing's ingenious solution involved alternating the application of fire and water to heat and cool the rocks, causing them to crack and become easily removable. This method enabled the creation of a 20-meter-wide channel in just 8 years.

The completion of the Dujiangyan system eradicated the perennial flood threat and transformed Sichuan into China's most fertile agricultural region. The resultant agricultural abundance provided the Qin State with a robust and reliable food supply, which in turn bolstered its economy and sustained its military endeavors. By stabilizing and enriching Sichuan, the Dujiangyan system fortified the Qin State's foundation, directly supporting its military campaigns and playing a significant role in their eventual unification of China. Thus, the Dujiangyan Irrigation System was not merely a case of public works; it was a decisive instrument of power.

If there is any credence to the concept of hydraulic despotism, China's version was born in Dujiangyan. The Qin used control over water resources to reward or punish communities, fostering dependence and reinforcing their authority. They could bestow irrigation benefits upon loyal communities, maintaining their rule, or strategically withhold water to exert pressure on dissenting communities, effectively punishing them to discourage resistance.

Looking toward the future, the global climate crisis is likely to profoundly affect the availability and predictability of water resources. This could have significant implications for political regimes historically associated with hydraulic despotism, such as those in the Middle East, Western United States, and Northern Africa. As water becomes scarcer, it may become a coveted resource, enabling rulers to exert greater control over communities, potentially exacerbating social inequalities and consolidating power.

Will the imperative to confront the global climate crisis drive innovation in new water management paradigms or trigger conflicts over dwindling resources? A paradigmatic shift toward centralized and integrated water governance becomes necessary when erratic and diminishing water flows render current fragmented and localized management approaches insufficient. This shift represents more than an operational upgrade; it is a fundamental reconfiguration of our relationship with water as critical infrastructure.

Centralizing water management demands a systemic approach, treating water flows—both physical and legal—as interconnected elements of a larger hydrological network. This requires comprehensive and strategic oversight to synchronize local needs with regional and global imperatives, transforming water into a vector of coordination that merges governance with technology. Yet, this centralization raises profound questions about control, access, and the emergence of new forms of hydraulic hegemony. The real challenge is in designing a water management system that is both resilient and adaptive, capable of accommodating the dynamic and unpredictable nature of water as a vital resource.

In contrast, decentralizing water management at the local level can be administratively disastrous in the context of a global water crisis. Managing a single river that sustains millions of lives across multiple jurisdictions—such as the Indus, Ganges, Amu Darya, Karnali, Nile, Euphrates, Tigris, Colorado, and Mekong Rivers—illustrates that decentralization or jurisdictional subdivision fails to address fundamental questions of water allocation. This is where governance, technology, and survival intersect, demanding a uniquely modern era of hydraulic despotism. Mitigating the risks of resource scarcity and conflict in an increasingly water-stressed, politically tenuous, and economically precarious world necessitates an integrated approach to governance to ensure viable water usage into the future. Such lessons are not without historical precedent.

YELLOW RIVER AND FALL OF THE QING

If the Qin unified China due to control of water, the dynastic rule collapsed due to administrative and hydraulic mismanagement. Two thousand years later, in the middle of the nineteenth century, China's last dynasty—the Qing—battled a combination of simultaneous challenges. Starting in the 1850s, the Qing had to manage "population growth, ecological degradation, opium consumption, landlessness, wealth inequality, and government corruption," which eventually led to "exacerbating social tensions and giving rise to acute episodes of tax resistance, popular unrest, and other troubles."[1] William T. Rowe, in his book "China's Last Empire,"

---

[1] Peter B. Lavelle, *The Profits of Nature: Colonial Development and the Quest for Resources in Nineteenth-Century China* (Columbia University Press, 2020), 4.

offers a comprehensive account of these various self-reinforcing factors calling China's nineteenth century the manifestation of a "perfect storm."[2]

Many have attempted to explain why the Qing bureaucrats were unable to respond to this "perfect storm." Thomas Rawski characterizes late nineteenth century and early twentieth century as one of global commercialization and technological development that brought a series of unprecedented political and economic challenges.[3] Within this framework, no single entity, including the state, held substantial significance. Others, like Gary Hamilton, paint the Qing as exceedingly weak and noninterventionist, administratively unprepared for a multitude of simultaneous challenges.[4] Narratives of bureaucratic weakness in the face of a polycrisis are convenient, but they miss the specific administrative dynamics of a bureaucracy under stress.

Kenneth Pomeranz's *Making of a Hinterland: State, Society, and Economy in Inland North China, 1853–1937* understands the Qing's failure beyond mere regime inaptitude. He examines the ecological and economic challenges of the Huang-Yun region (an area in Northern China at the intersection of the Yellow River and the Grand Canal, including the Western Shandong, Hebei, and Henan Provinces) during the mid-nineteenth century.[5] The book focuses primarily on water infrastructure, where much of the Qing legitimacy was concentrated in the eyes of "ordinary" citizens. Waterworks after all were the main responsibility of national authority, "central to two more broadly defined government tasks — the prevention of 'natural' disaster and ecological decay and the maintenance of infrastructure for transportation — that can rarely be handled by markets alone and that also set limits on economic integration."[6] As the most expensive area of governance, it served as a prime example of where the state first faced the limits of its purse strings.

<hr />

[2]William T. Rowe, *China's Last Empire: The Great Qing* (Harvard University Press, 2010), 7.

[3]Thomas G. Rawski, *Economic Growth in Prewar China* (Berkeley: University of California Press, 1989), 9–32.

[4]Gary G. Hamilton, *Zhongguo she hui yu jing ji*, Chu ban (Taibei Shi: Lian jing chu ban shi ye gong si, 1979), 120.

[5]Kenneth Pomeranz, *The Making of a Hinterland: State, Society, and Economy in Inland North China, 1853–1937* (Berkeley: University of California Press, 1993).

[6]Ibid., 25.

This became evident in 1852 when the Yellow River changed direction for the first time in 300 years, leading to constant flooding along the new 400-mile tract. Despite the Qing's technological capability and keen understanding of the region's needs, most of the resources were not directed toward fixing the pressing problem in Huang-Yun. Instead, the majority of state funding previously allocated to dike maintenance and flood prevention was directed to new modernization efforts along the coast. Pomeranz argues that "these interventions were not primarily determined by the greed, ignorance, or idiosyncrasies of particular officials but were governed by a systematic logic that itself linked economics and politics: its two central tenets were the need for more revenue to fuel the process of state building and the need to reduce foreign debt and the political pressures it creates."[7]

Despite the unprecedented nature of this crisis, the Qing administration possessed the expertise to address the issue.[8] The government had maintained the Yellow River for 300 years, which meant dealing with numerous floods and large-scale irrigation projects. In the 1880s, hundreds of Qing bureaucrats and foreign experts conducted feasibility studies. They drew up engineering plans using river training and flood-prone stone embankments, which would have fixed the course of the river and prevented future flooding.[9] Ultimately, the price tag for the new development project was deemed too high. Rather than a management problem, the Huang-Yun environmental crisis was a problem of priorities.

The critical factor responsible for the administration's failure to mitigate the challenges in Huang-Yun was the state's shifting focus toward other economic interests. While the hydraulic issues had increased post-1850s, at no point were they completely unmanageable. Funding for water works decreased significantly during that period. Some estimates note that "the central government's water conservancy outlays declined from 12 percent of total spending before 1850 to 3 percent between 1850 and 1900, then lower still to 1.38 percent in 1905."[10] Pomeranz aptly notes that what changed was the state's focus, which was now directing all

---

[7] Ibid., 19.
[8] Ibid., 274.
[9] Ibid., 215.
[10] Ibid., 167.

available resources to "national development, military strength, resisting foreign control, and escaping indebtedness."[11] In other parts of China, the Qing was reasonably successful in supporting infrastructure development and industrial modernization, but in order "to pay for this breakthrough, however, the state decreased its services elsewhere, leaving those regions to their own devices."[12]

The case of Huang-Yun exposes the limits of the conventional interpretation that attributes the failure to the regime's inherent weakness. In reality, Qing's inability to effectively address the ecological and economic problems in Huang-Yun resulted from a strategic redirection of state resources and the deprioritization of the region due to broader economic and political incentives toward the coastal regions.[13]

Peter Lavelle's *The Profits of Nature: Colonial Development and the Quest for Resources in Nineteenth-Century China* focuses on this particular shift of administrative priorities toward greater extraction. The expansion of the empire and the increasing population put a tremendous strain on China's natural resources and government funding. In response, the government sought to develop and extract as much wealth as possible from the newly conquered land. The book focuses on the career of Zuo Zongtang, a general and Qing bureaucrat who attempted to address the government's financial pressures with new irrigation projects and transfers of sericulture methods to Xinjiang. In this way, Lavelle builds on Pomeranz's work, by explaining specifically how Qing bureaucrats understood the hinterland and worked to revive the struggling state by creating new sources of revenue.

Addressing environmental issues and expanding production was seen as the core bureaucratic prerogative throughout the Qing administration. Government officials took the threat of crisis seriously, expounding the virtues of "natural profits of heaven and earth" (tiandi ziran zhi li), under which "helping people make use of the earth's resources was a core responsibility of any respectable official."[14] When Zuo became a government official, he committed to both developing the hinterland and making sure it was a useful contributor to the rest of the nation, implementing "measures to expand agrarian production, build hydraulic infrastructure, and

---

[11] Ibid., 168.
[12] Ibid., 210.
[13] Ibid., 272.
[14] Ibid., 7.

promote sericulture in Turkestani communities, seeking to boost the region's output of commodities."[15] Zuo and the national bureaucracy "printed and distributed concise farming handbooks ... seeking to propagate knowledge about techniques and tools for crop production" as well as subsidizing physical products like "plows ... cotton, rice, and vegetable seeds as well as mulberry seedlings and silkworm eggs to communities in Gansu and Xinjiang."[16]

This economic development came intricately tied to taxation and extraction. In order to get imperial funding, Zuo Zongtang ardently justified Xinjiang development projects to the Qing leadership, arguing that they "would lead to increases in total farmland acreage and invigorate rural economies, eventually boosting tax revenues and helping to ease the state's financial distress."[17] The Qing administrators of Xinjiang "surveyed and mapped lands and waterways, collating information about property size and productivity so that provincial officials could assess land taxes, verify land claims, and distribute unclaimed soil to migrants."[18] By 1878, Xinjiang and the military were producing enough grain with newly dug irrigation channels and imported technology that "long-distance grain transports were suspended and transport stations were shuttered, saving the imperial treasury a great deal of money."[19]

The multitude of crises at the end of the nineteenth century reduced the state's capacity in significant aspects, but it also motivated an important section of the bureaucracy to find new ways of extracting profits from nature to make up for the fiscal shortfall. As the Qing chose to deprioritize certain regions by focusing on others with more extractive potential, the source of fiscal troubles at the core of the dynasty remained a mystery.

It is clear that by the end of the nineteenth century, Qing coffers were empty: depleted by indemnity payments, niche modernization drives, and various internal military campaigns. Taisu Zhang argues in his 2023 book *The Ideological Foundations of Qing Taxation* that it is impossible to just look externally for answers to Qing financial weakness and its eventual

[15] Ibid., 9.
[16] Ibid., 10.
[17] Ibid., 169.
[18] Ibid., 9.
[19] Ibid., 119.

collapse. Rather, the answers lay inside of the bureaucracy, and "the missing ingredient is ideology."[20]

The Qing Dynasty remains a historic anomaly for one administrative nuance: China maintained the lowest tax rates of any empire on the planet. Taxing a mere 2 percent of the national production, it was a small fraction of Japan's 15–20 percent, England's 10–15 percent, France's 8 percent, or even the Ottoman Empire's 5 percent.[21] While many of these empires expanded their volume of agricultural taxes when the agrarian economy expanded, the Qing did not for almost 200 years. Despite some pretensions to the Confucian philosophy opposing burdensome taxation, the Qing is an extreme outlier in their low rate of agricultural taxes from all the previous dynasties. This was a significant financial strain because "the Qing economy was around 70–80 percent agrarian throughout its 268-year history, and until the dynasty's final few decades, the agricultural tax accounted for the lion's share of state income."[22] Zhang highlights this as the central problem of the Chinese economy, administrative weakness, and eventual divergence.

Within the entirety of the Qing fiscal system, the agricultural tax enjoyed a unique political status not afforded to non-agricultural taxes. The latter kept pace with the economic growth from the 1650s to the 1840s, the former, however, remained stagnant.[23] Particularly after the 1850s, Qing policymakers emphasize that agricultural taxes cannot be raised while commercial taxes can. The absolute volume of agricultural taxes remained locked in place until 1900, with a brief expansion in 1725 that triggered a large enough political backlash it can be considered an exception that proves the rule.[24] Simultaneously, the economy and the population more than tripled in that time. After the internal and external military challenges of the 1850s and the subsequent fiscal crisis, the Qing chose to only increase taxes on commerce and industrial production. This is the context within which Zuo Zongtang and the Huang-Yun administrators attempted to maximize industrial and mineral production.

Zhang points to the Ming-Qing transition as the answer to this historical and economic anathema. While peasant rebellions played an outsized

[20] Taisu Zhang, *The Ideological Foundations of Qing Taxation: Belief Systems, Politics, and Institutions*, 1st ed. (Cambridge University Press, 2023), 8.

[21] Ibid., 15.

[22] Ibid., 7.

[23] Ibid., 27.

[24] Ibid., 35.

role in the Marxist narratives of Chinese history, only one major dynasty was directly deposed by a peasant uprising: the Ming. The "Collected Writings About Statecraft from the Ming dynasty" (皇明经世文编) reflected on the moral wrong of agricultural taxation but never clearly articulated either the direct consequences or the possible harm of changes to the tax system.[25] Immediately after the collapse of the Ming, the Qing tone and substance against agricultural taxation radically changed.[26] The mid-Qing political writing could not be more clear about the harm. A series of government papers published throughout the nineteenth century all emphasized that the Ming had raised taxes beyond a reasonable limit and peasant rebellions deposed them as a result; if the Qing wants to avoid the same fate, taxes should not be raised above the red line (approximately 2 percent).[27]

Beyond a mere historical bias, the Qing commitment against raising agricultural taxes was institutionally self-perpetuating. The Qing was the only major dynasty in Chinese history to never conduct a nationwide land survey until its last five years, making tax hikes on peasants impossible.[28] Additionally, any proposal from regional bureaucrats to raise taxes on the peasants was met with instant reprisal and punishment.[29] The lack of revenue from the largest segment of the economy—that successfully provided funding for modernization to other empires throughout the world—left China in a continuously precarious economic position, forcing the bureaucracy to try everything from shipping silkworms across the empire to abandoning important flood-prevention infrastructure projects.

Perfect storms are not an anomaly; they are a feature of an anthropic universe. Starting in the 1850, the Qing Dynasty was certainly facing an unprecedented series of ecological, military, and social concerns. The dynasty's primary issue was not a lack of expertise, willingness, or capacity; it was a fiscal problem rooted in an ideological commitment to a limited political theory that became institutionalized for 200 years. Taisu Zhang concludes that "most importantly, Qing fiscal conservatism owed much of its political longevity to the fact that the state institutionally stopped land surveying ... thereby entrenching elite beliefs in Malthusian economic

[25] Ibid., 254.
[26] Ibid., 29.
[27] Ibid., 287.
[28] Ibid., 290.
[29] Ibid., 287.

decline ... as a result, mere informational inaction by the state is often sufficient to entrench preexisting ideological beliefs and can be just as politically manipulative – if not more so – than any direct ideological action it might take."[30]

BIBLIOGRAPHY

Hamilton, Gary G. *Zhongguo she hui yu jing ji*. Chu ban. Taibei Shi: Lian jing chu ban shi ye gong si, 79.

Lavelle, Peter B. *The Profits of Nature: Colonial Development and the Quest for Resources in Nineteenth-Century China*. Columbia University Press, 2020. https://doi.org/10.7312/lave19470.

Morin, Edgar, and Anne Brigitte Kern. *Homeland Earth: A Manifesto for the New Millennium*. Advances in Systems Theory, Complexity, and the Human Sciences. Cresskill, N.J: Hampton Press, 1999.

Pomeranz, Kenneth. *The Making of a Hinterland: State, Society, and Economy in Inland North China, 1853–1937*. Berkeley: University of California Press, 1993.

Rawski, Thomas G. *Economic Growth in Prewar China*. Berkeley: University of California Press, 1989.

Rowe, William T. *China's Last Empire: The Great Qing*. Harvard University Press, 2010. https://doi.org/10.2307/j.ctvjf9xsm.

Zhang, Taisu. *The Ideological Foundations of Qing Taxation: Belief Systems, Politics, and Institutions*. 1st ed. Cambridge University Press, 2023. https://doi.org/10.1017/9781108995955.

Jia, Shaofeng, and Dalong Li. "Evolution of Water Governance in China." *Journal of Water Resources Planning and Management* 147, no. 8 (August 1, 2021): 04021050. https://doi.org/10.1061/(ASCE)WR.1943-5452.0001420.

Li, Keke, and Zhifang Xu. "Overview of Dujiangyan Irrigation Scheme of Ancient China with Current Theory." *Irrigation and Drainage* 55, no. 3 (2006): 291–98. https://doi.org/10.1002/ird.234.

Willmott, W. E. "Dujiangyan: Irrigation and Society in Sichuan, China." *The Australian Journal of Chinese Affairs*, no. 22 (1989): 143–53. https://doi.org/10.2307/2158849.

Wittfogel, Karl August. "Oriental Despotism: A Comparative Study of Total Power," 1957. https://hdl.handle.net/2027/heb03224.0001.001.

---

[30] Ibid., 295.

Dam

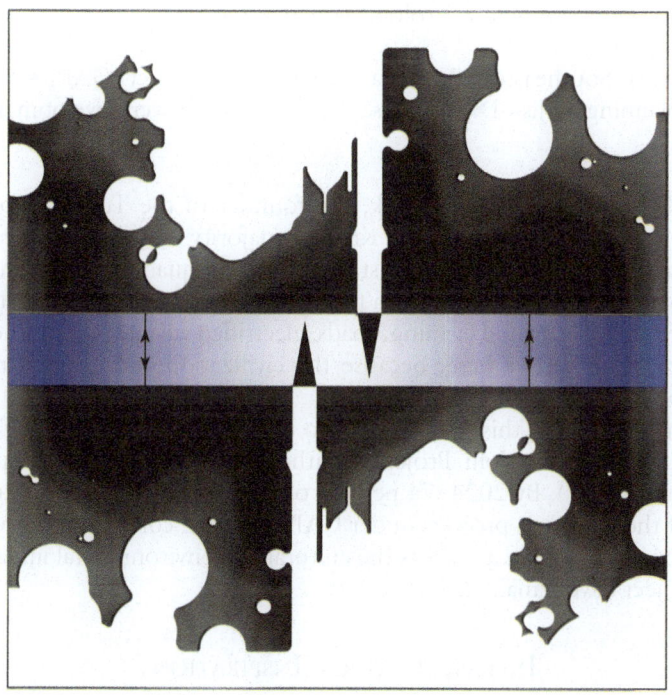

Hasankeyf by Flora Weil

R. Shemakov, *Centralized*,
https://doi.org/10.1007/978-981-96-2937-4_3

Abstract This chapter explores the Southeastern Anatolia Development Project (GAP), a transformative yet controversial infrastructure initiative aimed at revitalizing Turkey's Southeastern Anatolia region. Inspired by U.S. River Basin Planning models like the Tennessee Valley Authority, GAP sought to modernize agriculture, energy production, and social infrastructure through extensive dam construction and irrigation projects. While projects like the Ilisu Dam have contributed to energy generation, they have also resulted in significant cultural, environmental, and social costs, including the flooding of the ancient city of Hasankeyf and strained water-sharing relations with downstream neighbors of Iran and Iraq. The chapter emphasizes how major infrastructure projects often rely on cost calculations that fail to capture the full spectrum of long-term impacts, prompting questions about the trade-offs between nascent economic benefits and preservation in hydrological megaprojects.

Keywords Southeastern Anatolia Development Project (GAP) • River basin planning • Ilisu Dam • Hasankeyf • Hydropower development

In 1931, Mustafa Kemal Atatürk, the founder of the Turkish republic, visited Diyarbakır, the largest Kurdish-majority city in Southeastern Anatolia. Observing the region's stark contrast in quality of life compared to Western Turkey, he expressed a fervent desire to see it flourish: "I want to see factories, irrigated farming, roads, electrified villages, healthy homes, and evergreen forests here, because the civilization and life in Istanbul must be brought here too."

Forty years later, this vision began to materialize with the inception of the Güneydoğu Anadolu Projesi (Southeastern Anatolian Development Project, or GAP). By 2024, 74 percent of the energy projects and 26 percent of the irrigation projects under GAP had been completed. However, the economic benefits as well as the cultural and environmental impacts of the project have remained ambiguous.

INFRASTRUCTURAL INSPIRATIONS

GAP, in the spirit of many pan-national development projects around the world, was inspired in no small part by the United States. The project's utopian ambition of "placing another great civilization on top of all past civilizations in Anatolia" was primarily driven by River Basin Planning methods developed in the United States. This approach, focusing on developing an entire river's ecosystem, rather than a small tributary waterway, originated on the Mississippi River under the oversight of the Tennessee Valley Authority (TVA). Their work demonstrated a centralized administration's role in resolving competing water resource demands through cost-benefit analysis. In Turkey, the TVA model has been largely perceived as the ideal case of transforming a vast geography from a desert into a paradise.

Throughout the 1950s, the U.S. Bureau of Reclamation, the agency responsible for major public infrastructural works, trained Turkish engineers in American infrastructure development methods. Süleyman Demirel, one of GAP's founding fathers and Turkey's president from 1993 to 2000, drew much of his developmental aspirations for Turkey from a two-year program with the U.S. Bureau of Reclamation. Reflecting on his training, Demirel wrote, "I am the first Turkish engineer sent to the western states in the US by the government to enhance my knowledge and skills in 1949. There, I saw a lot and had the opportunity to apply them in my country. When I saw the [Hoover] Dam on the Colorado River in Nevada, I sat on a rock and watched it for three days."

Notably, Lake Mead, a reservoir created by that same Hoover Dam, has reached the lowest point in its existence due to the most extreme drought in 12 centuries, threatening to leave more than 40 million people without drinking water or electricity. As noted in Chap. 1, the infrastructure projects along the Colorado River, the world's most regulated stretch of water, have been widely criticized for causing significant environmental damage.

THE SOUTHEASTERN ANATOLIA DEVELOPMENT PROJECT (GAP)

The Southeastern Anatolia Development Project was first outlined by Turkey's Ministry of Industry and Technology in the 1970s. It included the construction of 22 dams and 19 hydroelectric power plants, projected to produce 27 billion kWh of hydroelectric energy annually and irrigate 1.7 million hectares of land. In the 1980s and 1990s, the project's scope expanded to cover education, transportation, and industry. Covering nine provinces in the Euphrates-Tigris Basin and Upper Mesopotamia plains,

GAP comprises 20 percent of Turkey's irrigable land and 33 percent of its energy potential.

Initially, the project's justifications emphasized historical legacy, economic opportunity, and social integration. The region's history as "home to the invention of the city, writing, the wheel, animal domestication, agriculture, irrigation, and similar groundbreaking developments" was often taken as reason enough to reinvigorate the region's economic output. In 1989, Ali İhsan Bağış described the project as a "rebirth of the prosperity which Mesopotamia enjoyed thousands of years ago, accompanied by modern technology." In 1993, Prime Minister Süleyman Demirel underscored the necessity of the GAP infrastructure to "activate the resources of a country and channel them to the welfare of the population." He argued that development required pairing resources with knowledge, science, and technology.

The cause of the region's "dormancy" was attributed to its residents, whose lifestyles were labeled as backward and ignorant by the Istanbul politicians. The 1999 GAP social action plan criticized the traditional social structures, including semi-feudal agriculture and nomadism, as barriers to social development. The plan admitted a lack of comprehensive engagement with the local population, favoring technocratic, top-down economic development methods to overcome perceived "backwardness."

In 2011, Turkey's Minister of Development Cevdet Yılmaz affirmed the utopian vision: "We march towards a GAP where we use our potential at a maximum level, where we build richer and better cities, where we have a more diverse and colorful environment with universities, civil society, media, and cultural activities, and where our people, especially our youth and women, participate much more in social and economic life."

The Ilisu Dam

The Ilisu Dam, envisioned as a key element of GAP, faced funding concerns and international pressure, delaying its construction. Journalist Mehmet Kizmaz explained that when construction began in 2006, several backers withdrew their support due to the project's environmental, cultural, and historical damage. The dam, completed in 2019, has since faced criticism from local and international observers in addition to downstream countries on the Tigris.

Standing at 135 meters high with a total water storage capacity of 10.6 billion cubic meters, the Ilisu Dam is Turkey's second largest and the world's largest by filling volume among concrete-faced rockfill dams. However, creating its water storage reservoir flooded the 12,000-year-old city of Hasankeyf. The Turkish government argued that the dam's 1200-megawatt power capacity, generating 4.1 billion kWh of electricity per year (approximately 3 billion Turkish Lira in annual revenue), justified the flooding and relocation of residents.

Despite these projections, estimating the dam's actual economic impact on the region is difficult. A 2014 MP from Hakkâri noted the skewed impact of development, accusing the government of intentionally planning to introduce wild capitalism to the region and shape a new identity. It is evident that the Ilisu Dam did not reduce inequality when considering that small agricultural enterprises cultivated only 10.5 percent of the land while large enterprises controlled more than half of the cultivable land.

The dam's investment structure also raised concerns. By 2010, loans from Turkish banks, backed by the government, funded the construction. The initial estimated cost of 2.5 billion Euros, which included 800 million Euros for expropriation and resettlement, likely exceeded expectations. Korkmaz added that the project left an economically lagging region even poorer. While the dam's economic benefits remain unclear, its ecological and social damages are evident. Residents lost vineyards, gardens, land, and homes to flooding. "Some 80 to 100 thousand people had to migrate," explained Ridvan Ayhan, a resident and activist. "They destroyed our history, our culture. This history is not only ours; it is the history of humanity."

The flooding of Hasankeyf has been central to the opposition. Ismail Can, head of excavation at Karahan Tepe, described the difficult trade-off: "We have destroyed thousands of years of cultural heritage for the sake of a dam. It is impossible to compare the cultural heritage of Hasankeyf with some income from the Ilisu Dam Hydroelectric Power Plant."

OPPOSITION AND CHALLENGES

Opposition to GAP was inevitable. In 2014, a Kurdish MP from Muş accused the Turkish government of making the region uninhabitable through large dams and hydroelectric power plants, destroying plant and animal diversity. Another MP from Şanlıurfa lamented the destruction of historical sites like Hasankeyf for electricity generation, arguing that the losses outweigh the gains.

Project planners dismissed such criticisms. An engineer for the State's Hydroelectric Works criticized activists for being "against everything," insisting that sacrifices had to be made. Another GAP engineer, responding to international criticisms, argued that Turkey's independent policies prompted Western opposition, which otherwise generously provided credit when Turkey's actions aligned with Western interests.

Others, like a former GAP coordinator, acknowledged the inevitable damages of development, admitting that infrastructure construction could have disproportionate impacts. The coordinator accepted that losses were part of development projects, noting that the goal was to increase the quality of life, even if it meant losing a generation in the process.

In 2002, a UK delegation released a report on the downstream effects of the GAP dams, highlighting significant changes in the Euphrates and Tigris Rivers' flow. Reduced flow caused increased salinity, affecting agriculture, and major adverse consequences for people in Syria and Iraq. The report accused Turkey of violating international conventions on water sharing.

With over 50 percent of regional water sources shared between countries, such accusations were damning. Iraq and Iran, heavily reliant on the Tigris, vocally opposed GAP and the Ilisu Dam. In 2018, the Iraqi Prime Minister accused Turkey of using the dam as a political instrument, noting that dams along tributaries had halved the water flow to Iraq. Iran's Foreign Minister also criticized Turkey's hydrology projects in 2022, calling them "unacceptable" and damaging to Iran's people.

Mehmet Kızmaz emphasized GAP's oversized international implications: "The Ilisu Dam had a very negative impact on the downstream Tigris River. Drinking water supply issues arose in many Iraqi cities, especially Baghdad and Mosul. Iraqi agriculture, largely based on river irrigation, was also at great risk. Iranian environmental organizations announced that the Ilisu Dam would exacerbate environmental issues and dust clouds from the drying Mesopotamian Marshes, destroyed by the dam."

GAP's vision of regional transformation has brought both financial reward and profound challenges, emphasizing the complexities of balancing development with cultural and environmental preservation.

BIBLIOGRAPHY

Bilgen, Arda. "The Southeastern Anatolia Project (GAP) in Turkey: An Alternative Perspective on the Major Rationales of GAP." *Journal of Balkan and Near Eastern Studies* 21, no. 5 (September 3, 2019): 532–52. https://doi.org/1 0.1080/19448953.2018.1506287.

Bilgen, Arda. "The Southeastern Anatolia Project (GAP) Revisited: The Evolution of GAP over Forty Years." *New Perspectives on Turkey* 58 (May 2018): 125–54. https://doi.org/10.1017/npt.2018.8.

Ilektra Tsakalidou. "The Great Anatolia Project: Is Water Management a Panacea or Crisis Multiplier for Turkey's Kurds?," *New Security Beat*, August 5, 2013. https://www.newsecuritybeat.org/2013/08/great-anatolian-project-water-management-panacea-crisis-multiplier-turkeys-kurds/.

Bilgen, Arda, et al. "Is the Glass Half Empty or Half Full? An Appraisal of the Four Decades of Turkey's Southeastern Anatolia Project (GAP)." In *Tigris and Euphrates Rivers: Their Environment from Headwaters to Mouth*, September 12, 2021. https://doi.org/10.1007/978-3-030-57570-0_82.

Pegram, Guy. *River Basin Planning: Principles, Procedures and Approaches for Strategic Basin Planning*. Asian Development Bank, 2013. https://www.adb.org/publications/river-basin-planning-principles.

Solomon, Erika, and Laura Pitel. "Why Water Is a Growing Faultline between Turkey and Iraq." *Financial Times*, July 4, 2018, sec. The Big Read. https://www.ft.com/content/82ca2e3c-6369-11e8-90c2-9563a0613e56.

Reservoir

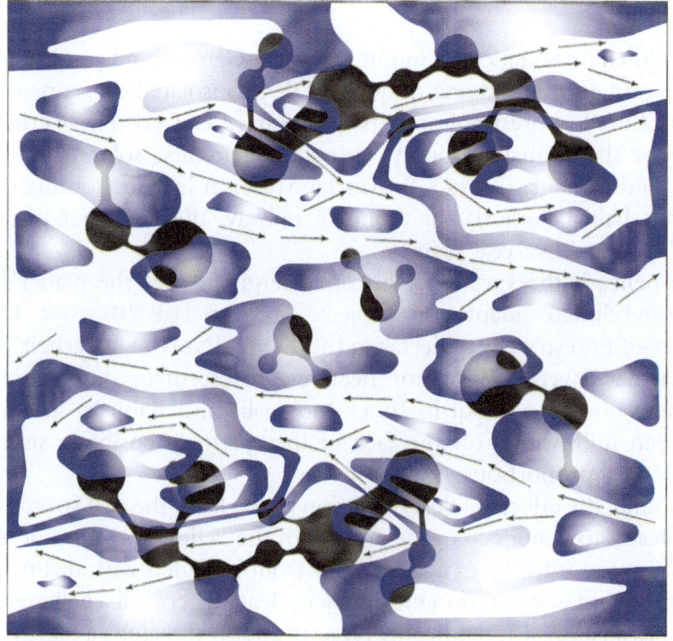

Gansu by Flora Weil

Abstract This chapter explores China's efforts to combat desertification, with a focus on the Three-North Shelterbelt reforestation project and the Hongyashan Reservoir in Gansu Province. These initiatives showcase the challenges and opportunities in balancing socio-economic development with environmental rehabilitation in arid regions. The chapter examines the ecological dynamics of desertification, the socio-economic pressures of population displacement, and the precarious interplay between human activity and natural systems. By comparing historical ecological losses, such as the drying of Lop Nur, the chapter positions desert ecosystems globally as interconnected landscapes, proposing a comparative methodology for managing aridity.

Keywords Three-North Shelterbelt • Reforestation • Hongyashan Reservoir • Lop Nur • Comparative desertology

In the global imagination, it might seem like Gansu stands on the periphery of world events. Judging only by GDP, this isolated desert province is one of China's poorest regions. Its spectrum of exports mirrors the complexity of the global economy: integrated circuits, solar panels, coal, apples, and cement. Gansu's Provincial Museum in Lanzhou luxuriously dedicates half a floor to the Longhai railway, the very first project of China's original five-year plan.

But beneath the surface of historic marginalia lies the planet's most ambitious climate adaptation project. For the last 40 years, China's Ministry of Forestry has undertaken the "Three-North Shelterbelt" initiative that has covered 70 million hectares of desertifying land with trees. Two deserts—the Kubuqi in Inner Mongolia and Babusha in Gansu—have been fully wiped off the face of the earth, ostensibly a success of mythological proportions.

In China, the effects of desertification ripple from the vast stretch of the Gobi Desert to major ecological arteries of the Yellow and Yangtze Rivers. Desertification introduces a cascade of troubles laden with distinct environmental and socio-economic impacts, leaving critical challenges that China has struggled to confront. Desertification threatens all fertile lands across China.[1] It is fueled by overgrazing, deforestation, and the overexploitation of water, coupled with extreme heat. The erosion of soil nutrients that comes with it significantly jeopardizes the country's food security. Because of this, the shadow of desertification threatens the livelihoods of local agricultural communities.[2]

Population displacement due to this escalating desertification represents an even larger challenge. Persistent degradation of fertile land has already triggered mass migration away from rural areas. People, in search of better prospects or government subsidies, are drawn toward freshly built metropolises. While China already struggles with the pressures of sustaining an enormous urban population, the influx from rural areas, stimulated by desertification, has further heightened the challenges. In most major cities, the sudden population surges have strained water, power, and transport infrastructure.[3]

Addressing these intricate issues, China has rolled out a variety of strategies aiming to mitigate the impacts of drought and desertification. This includes watershed management projects designed to better control and utilize water resources, even under changing climatic conditions.[4] Ecological restoration and reforestation initiatives have been launched to reverse the damage inflicted by desertification.

Minqin County, in Northwest China's Gansu Province, is on the frontline of the fight against desertification. The Hongyashan Reservoir, located in the county, is the largest desert reservoir in Asia. In the last few decades, it has become both a wall and an ecological corridor holding back the impending force of the deserts.

[1] Shilong Piao et al., "The Impacts of Climate Change on Water Resources and Agriculture in China," *Nature* 467, no. 7311 (September 2010): 43–51, https://doi.org/10.1038/nature09364.

[2] Asian Development Bank, "Managing Droughts and Water in the People's Republic of China," Text, Asian Development Bank, April 23, 2012, China, People's Republic of, https://www.adb.org/features/managing-droughts-prc.

[3] Ibid.

[4] Shaofeng Jia and Dalong Li, "Evolution of Water Governance in China," *Journal of Water Resources Planning and Management* 147, no. 8 (August 1, 2021): 04021050, https://doi.org/10.1061/(ASCE)WR.1943-5452.0001420.

HONGYASHAN

Completed in 1958, the Hongyashan Reservoir originally had a water surface of 25 sq km and a water storage capacity as high as 100 million cubic meters. During the peak periods, it irrigated 60,000 hectares of farmland and was the largest man-made reservoir in Asia.[5] Due to unpredictable climatic conditions there have been difficulties maintaining the reservoir. On June 28 of 2004, the Hongyashan Reservoir dried up for the first time in 50 years when sources feeding it suffered from decreased water flow.[6] The lack of water caused impactful shortages for local farmers and residents, killing the majority of plants, birds, and other wildlife in the region. A single instance of poor rainfall quickly upended an ecosystem.

In 2017, the reservoir's capacity was artificially increased by 148 million cubic meters to ease the rapidly worsening desertification in the lower reaches where the Badain Jaran Desert and the Tengger Desert connected. Without Hongyashan, 200,000 people would lose their livelihood.

The basin's water system has a peculiar relationship between surface and groundwater. Irrigation systems in the upper basin recharge the lower basin's groundwater, which re-emerges as springs, feeding downstream rivers. Intense agricultural development in the last decade supported rapid economic development but led to significant ecological and environmental issues.[7] The downstream Minqin Basin is now at risk of being buried by sand dunes, threatening an oasis community spread over 1000 square kilometers.

Since the 1950s, water inflow into the Hongyashan Reservoir has been diminishing. Data from cumulative curves indicates a notable increase in the impact of human activities, particularly irrigation, in Wuwei starting around 1975 and becoming increasingly significant over time.[8] Comparisons of historical and actual river discharges show that human activities led to a decrease of 40 percent, 49 percent, and 68 percent, respectively, in annual river flow during the periods of 1975–1980, the 1980s, and the 1990s.[9] In the Shiyang river basin, the evidence suggests

---

[5] Ibid.

[6] Ibid.

[7] Ibid., 28.

[8] Zailin Huo et al., "Effect of Climate Changes and Water-related Human Activities on Annual Stream Flows of the Shiyang River Basin in Arid North-west China," *Hydrological Processes* 22, no. 16 (July 30, 2008): 3155–67, https://doi.org/10.1002/hyp.6900.

[9] Ibid., 3166.

that climate change primarily caused upstream flow reductions over the last few decades. However, downstream flow decreases were mostly due to human activities. An increase in irrigation activity placed the reservoir at serious risk of running out of water.

Lop Nur

The history of China's greatest ecological loss, Lop Nur, hovered ominously in the background of Hongyashan. Lop Nur used to be a significant saltwater lake nestled at the confluence of the Tarim and Kongqi Rivers. With a maximum area exceeding 10,000 square kilometers, it was the second-largest saltwater body in China. The Lou-Lan Kingdom, which thrived from approximately 200 BCE to 330 CE, leveraged the lake's resources to become a critical trading and transportation hub along the Silk Road. This kingdom's prosperity, with its city sprawling over an area of 108,000 square meters, was intrinsically linked to Lop Nur's waters.

However, by the fourth century, the kingdom was in decline and succumbed to numerous converging adversities, including changed climate patterns, an alteration in river paths, incessant warfare, and outbreaks of disease. A significant contributor to this decline, as deduced from archaeological findings, was human activity, particularly the excessive cutting of Euphrates poplar trees for the construction of homes.[10] This deforestation led to a loss of water sources that the forests originally conserved, accelerating the lake's decline and the kingdom's downfall.

Despite the fall of the Lou-Lan Kingdom, Lop Nur persisted for an additional 1300 years. It sustained a substantial area of 3000 square kilometers as late as 1942. However, large-scale land reclamation and overuse of the water resources from the Tarim, Kongqi, and other rivers starting in the 1950s drastically reduced the lake's area to 660 square kilometers by 1962.[11] Eventually, by the 1970s, the lake had completely dried up, transforming into a desert.[12] This water misuse also negatively impacted the Tarim River, which lost a 300-kilometer stretch in its lower reaches. The river ceasing to flow led to the death of the poplar trees along its bank. In an effort to mitigate this environmental crisis, a water transfer program was introduced in the late 1980s to supplement the Tarim River and help

[10] Ibid.
[11] Ibid.
[12] Ibid.

resuscitate the ecosystem in Southern Xinjiang. This intervention led to the recovery of Taitema Lake, one of the downstream lakes along the Tarim River.

COMPARATIVE DESERTOLOGY

The Hongyashan Reservoir reflects the confluence of socio-economic progress and environmental conservation challenges posed by desert ecosystems. This reservoir, while playing a crucial role in boosting local agricultural productivity and fostering economic development, has ignited concerns about environmental degradation due to its hefty water consumption, especially for irrigation purposes. Understanding of this unique interplay between human endeavors and the desert environment not only reveals insights pertinent to the Gobi Desert but also contributes insights relevant to desert ecosystems universally.

With our planet's deserts collectively covering over a third of the earth's land surface, their environmental dynamics and underlying challenges present a compelling area for comprehensive and integrative study. Just as the Gobi Desert shares geophysical similarities with, say, the Sonoran or the Sahara, the ecological issues and human interactions within these landscapes present shared patterns and challenges. Considering our planet's deserts as part of a larger global system offers an opportunity to understand the recurring issues and parallel solutions across these environments. This holistic view is fundamental for devising inclusive and adaptable strategies that cater to the unique demands of these globally significant, yet often overlooked, ecosystems.

On the technological front, deserts can benefit from a mix of ancient and modern solutions. Traditional methods entail rainwater harvesting, check dams, and terrace farming. The indigenous populations in the Sonoran Desert, like the Tohono O'odham and the Hohokam, constructed stone and earthen structures to accumulate water during rains, which gradually infiltrated into the ground, replenishing groundwater levels. This process also curbed soil erosion, which is a key factor in desertification. The Hohokam also built check dams to slow water's flow, aiding in its absorption into the ground. Modern projects like Earthships in New Mexico demonstrate how greywater recycling systems in homes allow for the reutilization of water from baths, sinks, and washing machines for landscape irrigation.

BIBLIOGRAPHY

Campbell, Charlie. "China Pledges to Plant 70 Billion Trees in a Decade to Tackle Climate Change. Will It Work?" *Time*, May 25, 2022. https://time.com/6181214/china-tree-pledge-davos/.

Hao, Guzhuang, Fuping Gan, and Baikun Yan. "Remote Sensing Survey and Driving Force Analysis of Area Change of Hongyashan Reservoir in the Past Twenty Years." *Remote Sensing for Natural Resources* 33, no. 2 (June 2021): 192–201.

Huo, Zailin, Shaoyuan Feng, Shaozhong Kang, Wangcheng Li, and Shaojun Chen. "Effect of Climate Changes and Water-related Human Activities on Annual Stream Flows of the Shiyang River Basin in Arid North-west China." *Hydrological Processes* 22, no. 16 (July 30, 2008): 3155–67. https://doi.org/10.1002/hyp.6900.

Jia, Shaofeng, and Dalong Li. "Evolution of Water Governance in China." *Journal of Water Resources Planning and Management* 147, no. 8 (August 1, 2021): 04021050. https://doi.org/10.1061/(ASCE)WR.1943-5452.0001420.

Leung, Ka Ching. "Tackling China's Water Shortage Crisis." Earth.Org, July 23, 2021. https://earth.org/tackling-chinas-water-shortage-crisis/.

Li, Cheng, Yue Wang, and Guo-yu Qiu. "Water and Energy Consumption by Agriculture in the Minqin Oasis Region." *Journal of Integrative Agriculture* 12, no. 8 (August 2013): 1330–40. https://doi.org/10.1016/S2095-3119(13)60542-0.

Liu, Jiyao, Minjuan Zhao, Liuyang Yao, Wenxin Liu, and Gongyuan Fan. "Evaluating the Value of Ecological Water Considering Water Quality and Quantity Simultaneously." *Water and Environment Journal* 34, no. S1 (2020): 635–47. https://doi.org/10.1111/wej.12566.

Mischke, Steffen, Chenglin Liu, Jiafu Zhang, Chengjun Zhang, Hua Zhang, Pengcheng Jiao, and Birgit Plessen. "The World's Earliest Aral-Sea Type Disaster: The Decline of the Loulan Kingdom in the Tarim Basin." *Scientific Reports* 7, no. 1 (February 27, 2017): 43102. https://doi.org/10.1038/srep43102.

Moore, Scott. "How to Solve the Global Water Crisis." *Foreign Affairs*, October 30, 2022. https://www.foreignaffairs.com/articles/world/2018-03-20/how-solve-global-water-crisis.

Piao, Shilong, Philippe Ciais, Yao Huang, Zehao Shen, Shushi Peng, Junsheng Li, Liping Zhou, et al. "The Impacts of Climate Change on Water Resources and Agriculture in China." *Nature* 467, no. 7311 (September 2010): 43–51. https://doi.org/10.1038/nature09364.

Xie, Yaowen, Qiang Bie, and Chansheng He. "Human Settlement and Changes in the Distribution of River Systems in the Minqin Basin over the Past 2000 Years in Northwest China." *Ecosystem Health and Sustainability* 3, no. 11 (November 2, 2017): 1401011. https://doi.org/10.1080/20964129.2017.1401011.

Yang, Jianxia, Jun Zhao, Guofeng Zhu, Yuchun Wang, Xinggang Ma, Jianbang Wang, Huiwen Guo, and Yu Zhang. "Soil Salinization in the Oasis Areas of Downstream Inland Rivers—Case Study: Minqin Oasis." *Quaternary International* 537 (January 30, 2020): 69–78. https://doi.org/10.1016/j.quaint.2020.01.001.

Zhu, Q., and Y. Li. "Environmental Restoration in the Shiyang River Basin, China: Conservation, Reallocation and More Efficient Use of Water." *Aquatic Procedia* 2 (2014): 24–34. https://doi.org/10.1016/j.aqpro.2014.07.005.

Zhu, Xiaolin, Kwok Leung, Wing Li, and Lek Cheung. "Monitoring Interannual Dynamics of Desertification in Minqin County, China, Using Dense Landsat Time Series." *International Journal of Digital Earth* 13 (March 4, 2019): 1–13. https://doi.org/10.1080/17538947.2019.1585979.

Backbone

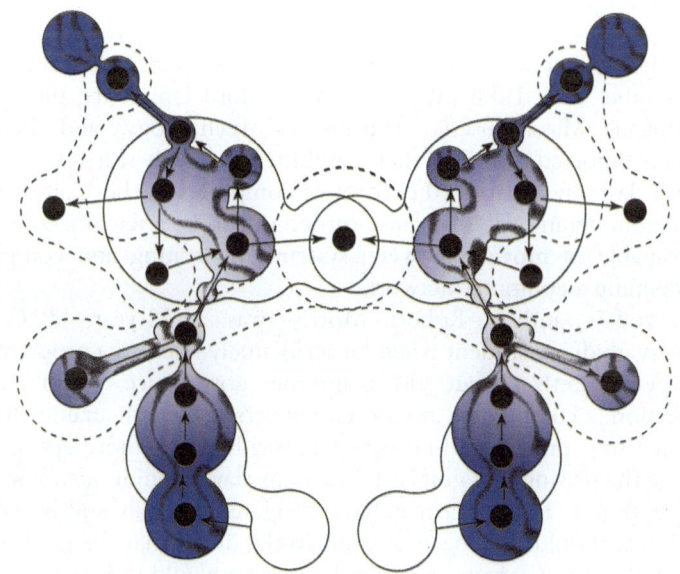

Morris Worm by Flora Weil

Abstract This chapter examines the legal impact of the 1988 Morris Worm incident on the development of global internet governance. As the first large-scale internet attack, the Morris Worm exposed critical vulnerabilities in the nascent internet infrastructure, catalyzing new bureaucratic and legal institutions. The chapter traces the historical roots of computing, the militarization of technology during the Cold War, and the rise of cybercrime, highlighting how security concerns shaped the internet's evolution. Through the lens of biological metaphors and institutional responses, it explores how the incident institutionalized cybersecurity frameworks, influencing global internet policies and the perception of the internet as both a vulnerable infrastructure and a tool for state control.

Keywords Morris Worm • Computer Fraud and Abuse Act (CFAA) • Cold war computing • Digital sovereignty • DARPA

A watershed moment for the history of the internet occurred at 11:28 pm on November 2nd, 1988. Academics at Stanford University, the RAND Corporation, Massachusetts Institute of Technology, and Berkeley University reported that all of their computers suddenly stopped working. Within 2 days, more than 10 percent of computers in the United States became nonoperational. The cause turned out to be a few dozen lines of code, capable of moving between systems, replicating and completely overwhelming a computer network.

The code's author—Robert Morris—was a 22-year-old Cornell University graduate student when he accidentally released a program that would permanently change global internet governance. In an internal investigation, a commission at Cornell University used an analogy to give semblance to a previously unimaginable incident: "A more apt analogy would be the driving of a golf cart on a rainy day through most houses in a neighborhood. The driver may have navigated carefully and broken no china, but it should have been obvious to the driver that the mud on the tires would soil the carpets and that the owners would later have to clean up the mess."[1]

---

[1] Ted Eisenberg, D. Gries, J. Hartmanis, D. Holcomb, M. S. Lynn, and T. Santoro. "The Cornell Commission: on Morris and the Worm." *Communications of the ACM* 32, no. 6 (January 1989): 706–709, 708.

Decades before the Morris Worm shut down much of the U.S. internet, academics, and military personnel predicted that the internet may become a revolutionary breakthrough, an ungovernable space that would liberate all social dynamics from constraints of the past. A 1964 article titled "The Computers of Tomorrow" imagined a future where computerized applications could be applied to "information retrieval, bill payments, and stock trading."[2] Despite the prophecies, the internet came to be defined primarily by insecurity and centralized control. Considering that the internet shares many features to hydraulic, energy, or transportation infrastructure, this shouldn't come as a surprise. Starting from the 1980s, the promise of a free telecommunication network was thwarted by the construction of legislative and bureaucratic boundaries. The history of the internet should be read as a culmination of expectations about security, contagions, and the Cold War political logic distilled into a familiar stretch of public works—infrastructure.[3]

The Morris Worm became the first large-scale internet attack and an inflection point that oriented the early internet around security concerns in the United States and around the world. As a public spectacle, the incident institutionalized centralization discourse within laws, courts, and security bureaucracies, shaping the global development of digital infrastructure to this day.

The Emergence of Computing and the Internet

During World War II, computing became deeply intertwined with military objectives. One of the most pressing challenges for the Allies was accurately targeting enemy aircraft with anti-aircraft artillery.[4] Early solutions depended on extensive mathematical tables known as "gun directories," which provided firing calculations for gunners. However, these manual methods were susceptible to human error and were too slow for the rapid pace of aerial combat.

To address these limitations, electromechanical devices were developed to quickly predict the future positions of enemy planes and automatically

---

[2] Martin Campbell-Kelly, and Daniel D. Garcia-Swartz. "The History of the Internet: The Missing Narratives." *SSRN Electronic Journal*, 2005, 21.

[3] Paul N. Edwards, *The Closed World: Computers and the Politics of Discourse in Cold War America*. New York: ACLS History E-Book Project, 2005, 7.

[4] Edwards, *The Closed World*, 45.

adjust the artillery's aim based on the directories' output. The mathematicians working on these battle alignment problems were commonly referred to as "computers."[5] Despite their expertise, they were still prone to calculation errors inherent in manual computations.

Recognizing the need for faster and more reliable calculations, the Department of Defense created the first autonomous circuitry computer— the Electronic Numerical Integrator and Calculator (ENIAC). Designed specifically to compute the "gun directory" one hundred times faster than was humanly possible, the ENIAC marked a significant leap in computing technology. Herman Goldstine, the director of the ENIAC project, noted that "the automation of this process was ... the *raison d'être* for the first electronic digital computer."[6]

Investment in the ENIAC continued to grow even after the war ended. In an address to President Roosevelt, Vannevar Bush emphasized that future military success would be determined by science rather than traditional infantry maneuvers:

> This war emphasizes three facts of supreme importance to national security: (1) Powerful new tactics of defense and offense are developed around new weapons created by scientific and engineering research; (2) the competitive time element in developing those weapons and tactics may be decisive; (3) war is increasingly total war, in which the armed services must be supplemented by active participation of every element of the civilian population.[7]

The urgency of the "competitive time element" became even more apparent in 1949 when the Soviet Union detonated its first atomic bomb.[8] To counter this new threat, subsequent American administrations restructured the bureaucracy to prioritize continuous scientific advancement and competition. This shift began with the development of the Semi-Automatic Ground Environment (SAGE) air defense system, which utilized computers for real-time control and the integration of multiple data sources.

By harnessing the full potential of universities, researchers, and civilian laboratories, the Department of Defense aimed to maintain technological

---

[5] Ibid.
[6] Ibid., 49.
[7] Ibid., 58.
[8] Martin Campbell-Kelly, *The History of the Internet*, 17.

superiority in all fields deemed militarily advantageous. From the 1950s through the 1960s, more than 25 military computing systems were designed based on the SAGE model.[9] This era saw the emergence of hundreds of university departments and private firms centered around the abundance of military contracts, solidifying the symbiotic relationship between computing advancements and military objectives.

As the Cold War intensified, so did the ambitions for scientific and technological advancement. In 1957, just one week after the Soviet Union successfully launched Sputnik into space, the U.S. government established the Advanced Research Projects Agency (ARPA). Its stated mission was to "keep the United States ahead of its military rivals by pursuing research projects that promised significant advances in defense related fields."[10] The rising fears of nuclear war—especially threats from outer space—provided the motivation for funding projects that had previously seemed untenable.

In 1964, Paul Baran, an engineer at the RAND Corporation, wrote a seminal article contemplating a worst-case nuclear scenario. He envisioned a communication system with no central authority that "would be designed from the get-go to transcend its own unreliability," enabling survivors to communicate safely across the country even after a nuclear attack.[11] This proposed network was markedly different from traditional telephone lines, where electrical signals flow in a single direction. Instead of sending information as one piece via a single cable, messages would be broken down into smaller packets, sent through multiple paths, and reassembled at their destination (packet-switching).[12] Baran articulated one of the earliest architectures for a national internet.

ARPA directors became increasingly interested in—and pressured to deliver—impressive scientific breakthroughs. Despite some historical narratives, Paul Baran was not the first to imagine what a packet-switching

[9] Christos Moschovitis. History of the Internet: a Chronology, 1843 to the Present. Santa Barbara, CA: ABC-CLIO, 1999, 34.

[10] Karl de Leeuw. The History of Information Security: a Comprehensive Handbook. Amsterdam: Elsevier, 2007, 745.

[11] Bruce Sterling. "Science Fiction And The Internet." Reading Science Fiction, 2008, 235–43, 239.

[12] Roy Rosenzweig. "Wizards, Bureaucrats, Warriors, and Hackers: Writing the History of the Internet." The American Historical Review, 1998.

network would look like.[13] Even before the RAND Corporation envisioned a nuclear-resilient communication infrastructure, networks existed
that allowed university researchers to temporarily use large computer systems located across the country.[14] In 1961, the Compatible Time-Sharing
System (CTSS) was developed at the Massachusetts Institute of Technology
(MIT), marking the birth of the first successful internet-based logic
system.[15]

The MIT campus also became a cultural hub for computing enthusiasts. The term "hacking" was originally used by MIT students to describe
elaborate physical pranks. In the early 1960s, this term migrated into the
computer science department, where it began to describe the unorthodox
approaches programmers used to solve complex problems.[16] This shift
linked the playful ingenuity of campus pranks to the innovative problem-
solving in computing, laying the groundwork for the modern usage of
"hacking" as a term for unauthorized intrusion into computer systems.

Emergence of Cybercrime

The idea of infiltrating computer systems without permission wasn't confined to academia. As early as 1966, the U.S. House of Representatives
held a week-long session to explore potential threats computers might
pose to privacy.[17] Although these meetings yielded few concrete results,
they attempted to address issues that would become critical as computing
technology expanded, such as the risk of adversarial intrusions. In a fore-
sighted turn of events less than two years later, West German authorities
arrested an East German spy caught accessing files at IBM's German
offices—a case some consider the first instance of computer crime.[18] While
this incident involved the spy physically inserting a disk into a computer,

---

[13] Ibid.

[14] Martin Campbell-Kelly, *The History of the Internet*, 24.

[15] Moschovitis. History of the Internet: a Chronology, 79.

[16] De Leeuw, *The History of Information Security*, 752.

[17] U.S. Congress, House of Representatives, Committee on Government Operations, *The Computer and Invasion of Privacy*, 89th Congress, 2nd Session, 1966.

[18] Michael Warner. "Cybersecurity: A Pre-History." *Intelligence and National Security* 27, no. 5 (2012): 781–99, 784.

researchers were already warning about the potential for remote unauthorized access.

Following this event, discussions about security and privacy intensified within government and organizational ranks. In October 1967, the Defense Science Board convened a study group to assess the risks associated with computing. The RAND Corporation released the classified findings in February 1970, forecasting that engineering solutions alone would not resolve computer security issues:

> Contemporary technology cannot provide a secure system in an open environment, which includes unauthorized users working at physically unprotected consoles connected to the system by unsecured communications. It is unwise to incorporate classified or sensitive information into a system functioning in an open environment unless a significant risk of accidental disclosure is acceptable.[19]

Throughout the 1970s, these insights shaped the approach to securing computer systems, emphasizing what Michael Warner referred to as "hygiene over hardware."[20] Consequently, most administrators prioritized measures like encryption, restricted access privileges, and hashed passwords to protect sensitive information.

Concerns about the government's relationship with the burgeoning computing industry began to mount during this period. When the National Bureau of Standards sought an encryption algorithm to secure government communications, IBM developed the Data Encryption Standard (DES) in collaboration with the National Security Agency (NSA).[21] This partnership was both fruitful and contentious. Fears arose that the NSA might have inserted a backdoor into DES, prompting a Senate investigation. Although the committee found no evidence to

---

[19] "Report of the Defense Science Board Task Force on Computer Security," Security Controls for Computer Systems, published by RAND for the Office of the Director of Defense Research, 1970 as cited in Michael Warner. "Cybersecurity: A Pre-History." *Intelligence and National Security* 27, no. 5 (2012): 781–99, 784.

[20] Ibid., 785.

[21] Albert Gersho. "Unclassified Summary: Involvement of NSA in the Development of the Data Encryption Standard." *IEEE Communications Society Magazine* 16, no. 6 (1978): 53–55, 52.

support these suspicions, the probe marked the first scrutiny of the inherent tension between the internet's openness, perceived vulnerabilities, and apprehensions about governmental overreach masquerading as protection.

The expansion of government-sponsored internet networks not only increased connectivity but also amplified worries about security. A significant leap in networking occurred when ARPA decided to interconnect the time-sharing projects it had nurtured at institutions like MIT, UCLA, Berkeley, and Stanford.[22] While numerous networking initiatives were underway globally, by 1978 the United States had devised a method to link these disparate systems. Advances in communication protocols enabled ARPA to facilitate interactions between systems using different algorithms or even operating on varied infrastructures.[23] These new standards gradually introduced computing and novel communication methods into the mainstream consciousness.

The advent of personal computers democratized internet access beyond academia's expectations. Utilizing the bulletin board system model, services like CompuServe and various BBS platforms became pioneering online communities, providing forums for enthusiasts to share information about the emerging computer world.[24] To illustrate the growing popularity, by the summer of 1984, CompuServe boasted 130,000 subscribers and operated 26 mainframe computers.[25] Although the internet had yet to achieve widespread mainstream adoption, a dedicated community of tinkerers and "hackers" began exploring the boundaries of permissible online access.

In 1984, one of the first cases of unauthorized computer access that validated the theoretical concerns of RAND researchers came to light. A group of high school students from Milwaukee, calling themselves by their area code—the 414s—used Telenet networks to infiltrate computers across the nation, including even unclassified military systems at Los Alamos National Laboratory.[26] The case quickly captured public attention.

---

[22] Martin Campbell-Kelly, *The History of the Internet*, 25.

[23] Fred Kaplan. *Dark Territory: the Secret History of Cyber War*. New York: Simon & Schuster Paperbacks, 2017, 53.

[24] Warner, *Cybersecurity: A Pre-History*, 787.

[25] Ibid.

[26] David Bailey. "Attacks on Computers: Congressional Hearings and Pending Legislation," *1984 IEEE Symposium on Security and Privacy*, Oakland, CA, USA, 1984, 181.

A congressional report from that year noted that the incident "was reported in virtually every newspaper and television news program in the country. Interviews were conducted on national television programs."[27]

Lacking clear legal statutes regarding computer access at the time, the case was enveloped in confusion. When a congressman asked Neal Patrick, the leader of the 414s, when he knew that they stepped out of bounds, Patrick responded: "When the FBI showed up at my door."[28] The case highlighted both the ambiguity in computer-related laws and the public's perception of the ethics surrounding unauthorized entry into foreign computer systems.

The widespread attention garnered by the 414s case demanded immediate answers. Media outlets across the nation directed criticism toward government administrators for the apparent security lapses. In September 1983, *The New York Times* reported on the growing concerns within the Department of Defense, highlighting doubts about the security of their 8000 networked computers.[29] Donald Latham, the Assistant Secretary of Defense for Command, Control, Communications, and Intelligence, acknowledged the issue, stating, "There'll be more of these hackers, and we're going to have to deal with their increasing sophistication."[30] Despite the alarm, none of the 414s hackers faced charges or sentencing for their exploratory intrusions.

During this period, legal institutions struggled to keep pace with the rapid emergence of computer crime. From the 1970s into the 1980s, most legal debates centered on analogies to traditional trespassing. Questions arose: Could information stored on interconnected and accessible networks be considered private property? Was unauthorized access to someone else's computer akin to entering their home uninvited? How significant was the perpetrator's intent in pursuing prosecution?

In the early 1980s, computer-related offenses were prosecuted under nearly 40 different statutes.[31] Minnesota led the way in 1982 by passing the first state law specifically addressing computer crime, though it

[27] Ibid., 182.
[28] Ibid.
[29] William Broad. "Computer Security Worries Military Experts." *The New York Times*, September 25, 1983.
[30] Ibid.
[31] John Montgomery. *White-Collar Crime: Fourth Survey of Law*. Washington, D.C.: Georgetown University Law Center, 1987, 23. The most common laws used to prosecute computer crime was the theft and federal mail fraud statutes.

primarily extended existing statutes on wire fraud, embezzlement, and theft to include computers.[32] It wasn't until the high-profile actions of the 414s that comprehensive federal legislation became unavoidable. Responding to mounting pressure to secure federal networks, Congress passed the Computer Fraud and Abuse Act (CFAA) in 1984. The virtual break-in by high school students into Los Alamos National Laboratory, coupled with intense media scrutiny and advocacy from the American Bar Association, spurred lawmakers to classify computer crime as a distinct legal category.[33] The CFAA addressed three specific areas:

> First, the Act made it a felony to knowingly access a computer without authorization in order to obtain classified United States military or foreign relations information with the intent or reason to believe that such information would be used to the detriment of the United States. Second, the Act made it a misdemeanor to knowingly access a computer without authorization to obtain information protected by federal financial privacy laws. Finally, it created a misdemeanor to knowingly access a federal government computer without authorization and thereby use, modify or destroy information therein, or prevent authorized use of such computer.[34]

The Act's limited scope reflected widespread skepticism about computers' role expanding beyond academic and governmental use. Immediate legal critiques pointed out its narrow definitions and limited applicability for prosecution.[35] An amendment in 1986 raised the criminal intent standard from "knowingly" to "intentionally," clarified certain terms, and introduced three additional offenses.[36] Nevertheless, its jurisdiction remained confined to cases involving federal interest.

---

[32] Ibid.

[33] *Computer Fraud and Abuse Act of 1986: Report (to Accompany H.R. 4712) (Including Cost Estimate of the Congressional Budget Office)*. Washington, D.C.: U.S. G.P.O., 1986. The Congressional Budget Office estimated that computer crime was causing financial losses between $145 million and $730 million annually.

[34] Susan M. Mello, "Administering the Antidote to Computer Viruses: A Comment on United States v. Morris," Rutgers Computer & Technology Law Journal 19, no. 1 (1993): 259–280, 262.

[35] Ibid., 257.

[36] Ibid., section (a)(3) was modified as only a trespass consideration. "Having accessed a computer with authorization" was replaced with "or exceeds authorized access." Three new offenses included "a felony provision for malicious damage to a federal interest computer, a felony provision for computer fraud, and a misdemeanor offense for trafficking in computer passwords."

For the first time, a prominent case ignited a national conversation about internet security with genuine federal urgency. In the wake of the Los Alamos incident, President Ronald Reagan issued the National Security Decision Directive (NSDD) to protect federal information systems. This directive swiftly expanded the National Security Agency's (NSA) responsibilities to oversee, research, and safeguard all "government telecommunications systems and automated information systems."[37] Testifying before a House committee, Donald Latham emphasized that "virtually every aspect of government and private information is readily available to our adversaries," warning that "unfriendly governments and international terrorist organizations are finding easy pickings."[38] Critics contended that the federal government leveraged the media-induced urgency surrounding the 414s to assert greater control over internet networks.

Many in Congress viewed these actions as governmental overreach. Between 1985 and 1987, multiple legislative efforts aimed to challenge Reagan's directive during meetings of the House Government Operations Committee. Representative Jack Brooks, one of the NSA's staunchest critics, described the NSDD as "an unprecedented and ill-advised expansion of the military's influence in our society."[39] A wide array of interest groups—ranging from the American Bankers Association to the American Civil Liberties Union—argued that the NSA's expanded role posed significant risks to the internet's future. These lobbyists urged Congress to restrict the Defense Department's authority to limit public access to online information on national security grounds.[40]

Through these debates, the 1980s began to define the boundaries of acceptable discourse regarding internet access, civil liberties, and the government's role in regulation. This period set the stage for future cycles of incidents prompting public panic and subsequent policy responses concerning internet security—a feedback loop that would recur in the years to come.

In the same year that the RAND Corporation's predictions became reality with the 414s hacking incident, another, even more alarming

---

[37] Warner, *Cybersecurity: A Pre-History*, 789.
[38] Linda Greenhouse, 'Computer Security Shift is Approved by Senate', *New York Times*, December 24, 1987. As cited in Warner, *Cybersecurity: A Pre-History*, 788.
[39] Ibid.
[40] Ibid.

security threat emerged. At a security conference at Lehigh University, Fred Cohen—a PhD student from the University of Southern California—demonstrated how a piece of code inserted into a computer system connected to the internet could spread to all other connected systems.[41] This demonstration was a pivotal moment, revealing the potential for malicious code to propagate unchecked across networks.

Two years later, in his doctoral dissertation, Cohen introduced the term "virus" to describe this phenomenon.[42] He defined it as a program capable of infecting other programs by modifying them to include a version of itself. He explained that such a virus could disseminate throughout a computer system or network by leveraging the access permissions of each user, infecting their programs in turn.[43] Each newly infected program could then replicate the process, causing the infection to grow exponentially. Despite the groundbreaking nature of his work, the concept of a computer virus didn't gain widespread attention until its existence "in the wild" was confirmed three years later.

Cohen's theoretical warnings materialized when a curious student with access to Cornell University's computer system unleashed a self-replicating program onto the internet. This incident not only validated Cohen's fears but also introduced new challenges for legislators and bureaucrats. The narrative of computer crime is complex—it's neither solely a tale of bureaucratic centralization nor simply a technological free-for-all. Instead, it is shaped by a myriad of factors: the militarized history of the internet, the anxieties of the late twentieth century, and the administrative battles over controlling a rapidly growing industry. These elements collectively influenced how security officials and the American public perceived internet security and the measures needed to protect it.

THE MORRIS WORM AND THE UNVEILING
OF NETWORK VULNERABILITIES

When the Morris Worm struck in early November 1988, it sent shockwaves through the computer science community. By the end of that decade, concerns about computer insecurity had been steadily growing

---

[41] Fred Cohen. "Computer Viruses: Theory and Experiments." *Computer & Security* 6 (1987): 22–35, 23.

[42] Ibid., 24.

[43] Ibid.

among researchers. The early 1980s had seen a mix of headline-grabbing computer attacks, popular films highlighting cyber threats, and various pieces of legislation aimed at bolstering computer security. However, the Morris Worm was different—it targeted the very institutions that had helped create the internet.

Within three days of its release, the worm had disabled more than 6000 government and university computers.[44] This self-propagating program was the first of its kind to operate autonomously after its creation. Unlike previous intrusions that required direct interaction with a computer's hardware, the Morris Worm spread on its own through network connections. It exploited vulnerabilities in three specific applications, and although it didn't directly harm operations, steal information, or delete files, it consumed so much system resources that infected computers could no longer perform other tasks.[45]

In just 15 hours, over 6000 computers—about 10 percent of all computers connected to the internet in the United States at the time—were effectively shut down. This included systems at critical locations like Wright-Patterson Air Force Base, the Army Ballistic Research Laboratory, and several NASA facilities.[46]

The creator of the worm, Robert Tappan Morris Jr., was a graduate student at Cornell University when he unleashed his creation into cyberspace. Adding an intriguing layer to the story, Morris was the son of Robert Morris Sr., a chief scientist at the National Security Agency's (NSA) National Computer Security Center and a contributor to the development of the UNIX operating system.[47] This connection fueled various conspiracy theories and intensified public interest in the incident.

An internal investigation at Cornell described Morris's actions as "a juvenile act that may simply have been the unfocused intellectual meandering of a hacker completely absorbed with his creation and unharnessed by considerations of explicit purpose or potential effect."[48] The ambiguous

[44] Larry Boettger. "The Morris Worm: How It Affected Computer Security and Lessons Learned by It." Global Information Assurance Certification Paper, December 20, 2000.

[45] Ibid., 15.

[46] National Computer Security Center, "Proceedings of the Virus Post-Mortem Meeting: ARPA/MILNET Computer Virus Attack," November 8, 1988, The National Security Archive, Washington, D.C.

[47] Fred M. Kaplan. *Dark Territory: the Secret History of Cyber War.* New York: Simon & Schuster Paperbacks, 2017, 60.

[48] Eisenberg, *The Cornell Commission,* 1.

nature of the worm led to debate over whether Morris should be condemned for his actions or thanked for exposing significant security vulnerabilities.

Clifford Stoll, a scientist at Harvard University who played a key role in combating the worm, encapsulated this dilemma during a presentation about the attack. His concluding slide posed thought-provoking questions: "Did this guy do us a favor by showing our vulnerabilities? Was it necessary? A month ago, the cover of *Time* magazine was about viruses!"[49]

Historians and experts have offered contrasting interpretations of Morris's intentions. Some emphasize the accidental nature of the worm's widespread impact, suggesting that Morris did not anticipate the extent of the damage it would cause.[50] Others place responsibility squarely on him for failing to foresee the consequences of releasing such a program.[51] A few narratives portray Morris as a well-intentioned explorer who took it upon himself to highlight security flaws after developers of the UNIX system allegedly ignored the vulnerabilities he identified.[52] One writer even suggested that Morris was seeking to establish an identity "to get away from his father's image and have one of his own."[53]

BIOLOGICAL METAPHORS AND THE RESPONSE
TO THE MORRIS WORM

In the wake of the Morris Worm attack, the federal government swiftly organized a conference just seven days later to grasp the full extent of the internet's security vulnerabilities. Coordinated by the National Computer Security Center (NCSC), the meeting convened experts from various

---

[49] Cliff Stoll. "Site Experience: Harvard," *The Morris Worm, 1988*, ed. Michael Martelle, Washington D.C.: The National Security Archive.

[50] Josephine Wolff. *You'll See This Message When It Is Too Late: the Legal and Economic Aftermath of Cybersecurity Breaches.* Cambridge: MIT Press, 2018. And Christos Moschovitis. *History of the Internet: a Chronology, 1843 to the Present.* Santa Barbara, CA: ABC-CLIO, 1999.

[51] Ted Eisenberg, Gries, J. Hartmanis, D. Holcomb, M. S. Lynn, and T. Santoro. "The Cornell Commission: on Morris and the Worm." Communications of the ACM 32, no. 6 (January 1989) and Karl Leeuw. The History of Information Security: a Comprehensive Handbook. Amsterdam: Elsevier, 2007.

[52] Moschovitis. *History of the Internet*, 78.

[53] Larry Boettger. "The Morris Worm: How It Affected Computer Security and Lessons Learned by It." Global Information Assurance Certification Paper, December 20, 2000.

security agencies, internet operations, and academic institutions.[54] Representatives from the Air Force, Army, Defense Advanced Research Projects Agency (DARPA), National Security Agency (NSA), Federal Bureau of Investigation (FBI), National Institute of Standards and Technology (NIST), and scholars from Harvard, Berkeley, MIT, and Stanford brought their unique perspectives and interests to the table.[55] Their discussions revealed how deeply biological language had permeated technical systems, with the internet often described as a living organism and the experts as doctors poised to heal it. This metaphorical framing allowed them to imbue their work with social significance, casting computers, the internet, and national security "to be articulated in the idiom of organic nature, an idiom that can often obscure the historical and cultural specificity of such conceptions."[56]

From the outset, computers were almost exclusively regarded in biological terms. William Sherlin, speaking for the Defense Advanced Research Projects Agency (DARPA), structured his presentation with subheadings reminiscent of a medical textbook:

1. THE VIRUS
2. SYMPTOMS AND BEHAVIOR
3. METHOD OF ATTACK
4. ESTABLISHING THE INFECTION
5. DETECTION AND DIAGNOSIS
6. IMMUNIZATION AND PREVENTION
7. ASSESSMENT AND RECOVERY[57]

The DARPA team fully embraced the notion of a living virus, extending the metaphor to describe the cyber threat. They noted that "the principal symptom of the virus ... is degradation of system responses."[58] Here, the computer code itself, detached from its creator, was endowed with

---

[54] National Computer Security Center, "Proceedings of the Virus Post-Mortem Meeting: ARPA/MILNET Computer Virus Attack," November 8, 1988, The National Security Archive, Washington, D.C, 7.

[55] Ibid.

[56] Stefan Helmreich. "Flexible Infections: Computer Viruses, Human Bodies, Nation-States, Evolutionary Capitalism." *Science, Technology, & Human Values* 25, no. 4 (2000): 472–91, 474.

[57] William Scherlis and Stephen Squires, "Memorandum for the Director," *The Morris Worm, 1988,* ed. Michael Martelle, Washington D.C.: The National Security Archive, 8.

[58] Ibid, 9.

agency: "The principal activity of the virus is to replicate itself and spread to other machines … with resultant degradation of performance."[59]

Michael Muuss of the U.S. Army Ballistic Research Laboratory (BRL) took the metaphor even further by defining a virus as: "From Latin: slimy liquid, poison, stench … Complex molecules, capable of growth and multiplication only in living cells."[60] In this portrayal, the viral contagion appeared imminent and autonomous, lacking a specific subject or source, driven solely by a goal of destruction.

In a scenario where malicious code aims for "infection," the defenders saw themselves as first responders ready to administer an antidote. The DARPA researchers assured attendees that "immunization and/or prevention measures were developed."[61] Muuss affectionately dubbed his scientists the "antiviral team" and management the "virus busters."[62] The underlying message was clear: only experts with the right tools and knowledge could thwart the danger the virus posed to the collective health of the internet.

An atmosphere of public spectacle surrounded many of the BRL presentations. The final report from the NCSC emphasized the need for "a single U.S. government focal point at the national level to interact with the press."[63] While the editors stressed efficient and coordinated messaging, some presenters were wary of inciting public panic. Anticipating that his biological metaphors might be too provocative, Muuss quipped, "My fear: these headlines: 'Computer Virus Spreads to Humans: 96 left dead …'".[64]

The construction of the internet as a vulnerable body is significant because it influences the solutions these metaphors imply. Contagion metaphors related to the internet are closely tied to the bodily anxieties of the twentieth century. When virology emerged as a field during the era of McCarthyism, viruses "increasingly assumed the characteristics of communists; they were devious and sinister, forming a kind of fifth column."[65] This model of a healthy body fighting off infection carries assumptions about sovereignty, foreignness, and immunity.

---

[59] Ibid.

[60] Michael Muuss, "Site Experience: Army Ballistic Research Lab," *The Morris Worm, 1988*, ed. Michael Martelle, Washington D.C.: The National Security Archive, 5.

[61] Sherlis, *Memorandum for the Director*, 9.

[62] Muuss, *Site Experience*, 8.

[63] National Computer Security Center, *Proceedings of the Virus Post-Mortem*, 89.

[64] Muuss, *Site Experience*, 17.

[65] Zahi Zalloua and Bruce A. Magnusson. *Contagion: Health, Fear, Sovereignty*. Seattle and London: University of Washington Press, 2012, 43.

Such framing demands "enormous quantities of centrally, if not globally, managed funds and research, as well as the institutionalization of global biopolitical strategies of surveillance, diagnosis, containment, eradication, and therapy."[66] Consequently, a backbone of vigilance is established, turning every internet user into a potential vector for viral contagion.[67] The NCSC experts were inadvertently mobilizing fear and anxiety, recognizing that these emotions needed to permeate public discourse to effectively address the threat.

The discussions about computer viruses, internet vulnerabilities, and concepts of viral immunity soon extended far beyond the closed meetings of the NCSC. Many of the experts who participated in these gatherings went on to provide legal counsel, advise members of Congress, and lead major cybersecurity firms. The rhetoric of contagion and immunological metaphors had a profound impact—not only on court decisions and internet legislation across the country but also on how American citizens interacted with their computers. The Morris Worm incident became a catalyst, bringing private conversations among computer experts about perceived internet vulnerabilities into the public sphere. This spillover had lasting effects on legislation, legal precedents, and the burgeoning computer security industry.

JUDICIAL, LEGISLATIVE, AND BUREAUCRATIC SPILLOVER

Three years after the passage of the Computer Fraud and Abuse Act (CFAA) in 1986, Robert Tappan Morris became the first person prosecuted under its provisions. The Northern District of New York indicted Morris on misdemeanor and felony charges, citing sections of the Act that addressed:

> *Intentionally access[ing] a Federal interest computer without authorization, and by means of one or more instances of such conduct alter[ing], damag[ing], or destroy[ing] information in any such Federal interest computer, or prevent[ing] authorized use of any such computer or information, and thereby (A) caus[ing] loss to one or more others of a value aggregating $1000 or more during any one year period.*[68]

---

[66] Ibid., 6.
[67] Stefan Elbe. "Bodies as Battlefields: Toward the Medicalization of Insecurity." *International Political Sociology* 6, no. 3 (2012): 320–332, 323.
[68] Camille Marion, "Computer Viruses and the ,Law," Dickinson Law Review 93, no. 3 (Spring 1989): 625–642, 630.

Morris's defense contested these allegations, arguing that under the law "he not only had to intentionally access a federal interest computer, but he also had to intend to prevent authorized use of those computers."[69] They maintained that Morris did not exceed his authorized access as a student with full privileges on Cornell University's computer networks and did not intend to cause damage, especially since he attempted to release a fix for the worm. The district judge, however, deemed the CFAA "unambiguous" and ruled that legislative history was unnecessary. He decided against Morris, stating that the intent requirement did not apply to the damage clause.[70]

The appellate court viewed the Act's clarity differently. They scrutinized the case, focusing on the ambiguity introduced by punctuation—specifically, whether "intentionally" applied only to the "access" clause or also included the "damage" clause. After reviewing the legislative history, the appellate court agreed with the district court's conclusion: only the intent to access without authorization was necessary for prosecution under the CFAA.

The prosecution of Morris became a landmark case for future computer crime litigation. Although the Supreme Court declined to hear the case without comment, the appellate decision set two crucial legal precedents. First, it established that the minimum requirement for prosecution under the CFAA was intentional unauthorized access, regardless of intent to cause damage. Second, it solidified the definition of an "outsider" as anyone who uses a computer program or accesses a network without proper authorization, effectively creating a legal boundary around each individual computer system and program.[71] Judge Jon Newman articulated this point in his ruling:

> Morris did not use either of those features [the email and directory applications] in any way related to their intended function. He did not send or read mail nor discover information about other users; instead, he found holes in both programs that permitted him a special and unauthorized access route into other computers.[72]

---

[69] Susan M. Mello, "Administering the Antidote to Computer Viruses: A Comment on United States v. Morris," Rutgers Computer & Technology Law Journal 19, no. 1 (1993): 259–280, 263.

[70] Ibid., 268.

[71] Ibid., 271.

[72] Josephine Wolff. You'll See This Message When It Is Too Late: the Legal and Economic Aftermath of Cybersecurity Breaches. Cambridge: MIT Press, 2018, 213.

The crux of the matter wasn't whether Morris had permission from the university to experiment with the programs; it was that the creators of the exploited software did not intend for users to interact with their applications in the manner that Morris did.

Sentencing in the Morris case also broke new ground. The prosecution sought a 27-month prison term, while the defense argued for 6 months. The judge acknowledged the challenge of setting a precedent for sentencing in such a novel area of law, noting that "the dollar loss overstates the seriousness of the offense."[73] Privately, critics expressed unease; one remarked, "If a person hasn't acted with malicious intent, it's not quite clear what you're trying to deter."[74] Ultimately, the judge decided that to discourage future hackers from unauthorized access, Morris would receive 3 years of probation, 400 hours of community service, and a fine of $10,050.[75]

The Morris Worm incident propelled discussions about computer viruses into the halls of Congress. Much like the 414s hacking group had spurred the creation of the 1986 legislation, Morris's actions ushered in a new era of discourse on cyber threats. As the attacks captured national attention, the Senate Judiciary Committee formed a Subcommittee on Technology and the Law, which began holding hearings on "Computer Viruses" in May 1989.[76] During the first panel's testimony, William Sessions, the Director of the Federal Bureau of Investigation (FBI), highlighted the shortcomings of the CFAA, becoming the first to officially use the term "virus" in this context:

> Existing criminal statutes, however, are not specific on the question of whether unauthorized access is a crime where no theft or damage occurs, and there is no statute specifically addressing viruses. Current criminal statutes, by and large, address the issue of computers as the vehicle of the crime ... We have seen an increase in crimes in which the computer or computerized information is the target of the crime. Computer viruses present

---

[73] Mello, *Administering the Antidote*, 275.

[74] Marc Rotenberg, Office Director of Computer Professionals for Social Responsibility, *quoted in* Susan M. Mello, "Administering the Antidote to Computer Viruses: A Comment on United States v. Morris," Rutgers Computer & Technology Law Journal 19, no. 1 (1993): 259–280.

[75] Ibid., 275.

[76] U.S. Congress, Senate, Judiciary Subcommittee on Technology and Law, *Hearings on Computer Viruses*, 101 Congress, 1st session, May 15, 1989.

one such example ... With today's technology, viruses can begin the infectious process from a home personal computer, an office, an academic institution, or from almost anywhere in the world.[77]

The court case and congressional hearings marked the beginning of a new chapter in computer crime legislation. The Morris Worm incident spotlighted the inadequacies of existing computer laws, which had been crafted without anticipating that internet technology would extend beyond military and scientific communities. Discussions about computer insecurity, which had been circulating among specialists since as early as 1966, finally found an official platform due to the high-profile nature of Morris's unintended experiment. This is how the collective security imagination, reinforced by rhetorical metaphors and the institutional needs of computer scientists and investigative agencies, significantly contributed to the securitization of computer networks.

Following the Morris Worm, computer crime started to pique international attention. In 1989, the Council of Europe published a report urging countries to create a unified set of principles to ensure an efficient response to cybercrime.[78] As more countries began to seriously adopt internet protocols, a push for legal standardization accelerated. In 1990, the United Nations' Congress on the Prevention of Crime and the Treatment of Offenders called on countries to "combat cybercrime by modernizing their law, improving computer security and promoting a comprehensive international framework of standards for preventing, prosecuting, and punishing computer related crime."[79]

BUREAUCRATIC INTERVENTION AND THE INSTITUTIONALIZATION OF CYBERSECURITY

In the aftermath of the Morris Worm incident, the process of medicalizing computer security led academics and officials to advocate for a comprehensive approach to protecting national networks. By constructing the virus as a disembodied threat, the resulting top-down panic underscored

---

[77] U.S. Congress, Senate, Judiciary Subcommittee on Technology and Law, *Hearings on Computer Viruses,* 101 Congress, 1st session, May 15, 1989 (opening testimony of William Sessions).

[78] Susan Brenner. "History of Computer Crime." In *The History of Information Security,* 1st ed., 705–21. Elsevier Science, 2007, 715.

[79] Ibid.

the need for an orchestrated and efficient response. Recommendations from the National Computer Security Center's (NCSC) post-mortem meeting outlined the blueprint for institutions that would coordinate the security of the increasingly nationalized internet. This meeting gave birth to two entities that continue to influence computer security today: the Computer Emergency Response Team (CERT) and the commercialization of cybersecurity.

The NCSC meeting identified the decentralized network of computer scientists who had played a crucial role in combating the worm. Those invited were not only the affected parties but also the source of the solution. Academics from Harvard, Berkeley, MIT, Stanford, and other institutions were collectively termed the "old boy network"—a label reflecting both the demographics of computer science at the time and the close relationships between government agencies and academic research circles.[80] One key recommendation emphasized the need to centralize and maintain "technical relationships with the computer science 'old boy network,'" stressing that their "consensus, support, and trust is required" for government security initiatives.[81] These connections often blurred the lines between scientists as independent actors and their roles within governmental frameworks, positioning them as the vanguard for securing American networks.[82]

Coordination between researchers and the military was swiftly institutionalized. Recognizing that an informal network of experts was insufficient, the NCSC's foremost recommendation called for establishing a "centralized coordination center" managed by the NSA and NIST. This center would serve as a "place to report problems and request solutions," with the potential to evolve into a "national-level command center supporting the government and private sector alike."[83] Just a month later, DARPA established the Computer Emergency Response Team (CERT) at Carnegie Mellon University to coordinate nationwide network security. Beyond being a repository of expertise, CERT became responsible for

---

[80] National Computer Security Center, "Proceedings of the Virus Post-Mortem Meeting: ARPA/MILNET Computer Virus Attack," November 8, 1988, The National Security Archive, Washington, D.C, 95.

[81] Ibid.

[82] Wolfe. *Freedoms Laboratory*, 13.

[83] National Computer Security Center, "Proceedings of the Virus Post-Mortem Meeting: ARPA/MILNET Computer Virus Attack," November 8, 1988, The National Security Archive, Washington, D.C, 95.

"reporting incidents, conducting security research, and educating the computer user community about security issues."[84] Funded by the Department of Defense, CERT initially focused on ARPANET and MILNET, highlighting the government's priority on federally significant networks. Anticipating future needs, DARPA's press release predicted that "each major computer community may decide to establish its own CERT"—a forecast that soon materialized.[85]

The Morris Worm incident served as a catalyst, bringing previously insular discussions about contagion metaphors into the public sphere. Through legal reforms and industry initiatives, concepts of a digital nation, immunity, and medicalization became entrenched in cybersecurity discourse. The laws enacted after the Morris incident helped define the internet before it achieved widespread popularity in the 1990s. While researchers had been aware of infrastructure vulnerabilities since the 1960s, it was this high-profile incident that solidified a framework of legal structures to address institutional anxieties.

It's essential to recognize the contingent elements introduced by Morris's actions. The enforcement of the Computer Fraud and Abuse Act (CFAA), which shifted security responsibility from program designers to users, contributed both to the rapid growth of the internet and its tendency to scapegoat the computer experts. The narrative of internet security is as much a rhetorical construction as it is a technical one. Designed with inherent insecurities, the internet's early guardians laid the foundation for an "infrastructure of surveillance, vigilance, and counter-epidemic action," making anxiety a driving force behind its global expansion.[86] Yet, even as the internet exists in a state of perpetual emergency, true immunity remains elusive. To defend it from external threats encroaching on its freedom, the internet itself must be quarantined, protected, and monitored.

GLOBAL IMPLICATIONS AND ONGOING CHALLENGES

The constraints imposed by American technological policies do not stop at national borders. Significant dilemmas arise when considering how domestic rhetoric extends beyond the United States. As early as 1996, Russian

---

[84] Laura DeNardis. "A History of Internet Security." In *The History of Information Security*, 1st ed., 681–704. Elsevier Science, 2007, 685.

[85] Ibid., 686.

[86] Zalloua, *Contagion: Health, Fear, Sovereignty*, 6.

and Chinese leaders expressed concerns about the connections between American security agencies and exported infrastructure. In a 1996 *Pravda* interview, a general from the Russian Chamber of Trade and Commerce remarked:

> Many people are happy that they got access to the Internet Web, but the owners are American, not us. Now in Russia lots of American servers have been set up, and they supply their equipment for low prices ... We must remember about the 'logical bombs' inlaid in their programs. Can you imagine what would happen if one day on a special command all the equipment will be paralyzed.[87]

Similar apprehensions were voiced in a 1996 article in the *Liberation Army Daily*, highlighting concerns about new communication networks: "An information war is inexpensive, as the enemy country can receive a paralyzing blow through the Internet, and the party on the receiving end will not be able to tell whether it is a child's prank or an attack from its enemy."[88] Chinese and Russian officials echoed the same worries that U.S. Congress members, academics, and security experts had been articulating since the 1970s.

BIBLIOGRAPHY

Bailey, David. "Attacks on Computers: Congressional Hearings and Pending Legislation," *1984 IEEE Symposium on Security and Privacy*, Oakland, CA, USA, 1984.

Broad, William. "Computer Security Worries Military Experts." *New York Times*, September 25, 1983a.

Cohen, Fred. "Computer Viruses: Theory and Experiments." *Computer & Security* 6 (1987a): 22–35.

Computer Fraud and Abuse Act of 1986: Report (to Accompany H.R. 4712) (Including Cost Estimate of the Congressional Budget Office). Washington, D.C.: U.S. G.P.O., 1986a.

Eisenberg, T., D. Gries, J. Hartmanis, D. Holcomb, M. S. Lynn, and T. Santoro. "The Cornell Commission: on Morris and the Worm." *Communications of the ACM* 32, no. 6 (January 1989a): 706–9.

---

[87] Warner, *Cybersecurity: A Pre-History*, 791.
[88] Ibid.

Muuss, Michael. "Site Experience: Army Ballistic Research Lab," *The Morris Worm, 1988,* ed. Michael Martelle, Washington D.C.: The National Security Archive.

National Computer Security Center, "Proceedings of the Virus Post-Mortem Meeting: ARPA/MILNET Computer Virus Attack," November 8, 1988, The National Security Archive, Washington, D.C.

Scherlis, William and Stephen Squires, "Memorandum for the Director," *The Morris Worm, 1988,* ed. Michael Martelle, Washington D.C.: The National Security Archive.

Stoll, Clifford. "Site Experience: Harvard," *The Morris Worm, 1988,* ed. Michael Martelle, Washington D.C.: The National Security Archive

U.S. Congress, House of Representatives, Committee on Government Operations, *The Computer and Invasion of Privacy,* 89th Congress, 2nd Session, 1966.

U.S. Congress, Senate, Judiciary Subcommittee on Technology and Law, *Hearings on Computer Viruses,* 101 Congress, 1st session, May 15, 1989a (written statement of Clifford Stoll).

U.S. Congress, Senate, Judiciary Subcommittee on Technology and Law, *Hearings on Computer Viruses,* 101 Congress, 1st session, May 15, 1989b (opening testimony of William Sessions).

U.S. Library of Congress, Congressional Research Service, *Comprehensive National Cybersecurity Initiative: Legal Authorities and Policy Considerations,* by John Rollins and Anna Henning, 2009.

Bell, Colleen. "War and the Allegory of Medical Intervention: Why Metaphors Matter." *International Political Sociology* 6, no. 3 (2012): 325–28.

Brenner, Susan. "History of Computer Crime." *The History of Information Security,* 1st ed., Elsevier Science, 2007a, pp. 705–721.

Boettger, Larry. "The Morris Worm: How It Affected Computer Security and Lessons Learned by It." Global Information Assurance Certification Paper, December 20, 2000.

Borradori, Giovanna. *Philosophy in a Time of Terror: Dialogues with Jürgen Habermas and Jacques Derrida.* Univ. of Chicago Press, 2009.

Broad, William. "Computer Security Worries Military Experts." *New York Times,* 25 Sept. 1983b.

Cavelty, Myriam Dunn. *Cyber-Security and Threat Politics: US Efforts to Secure the Information Age.* London: Routledge, 2009.

Campbell-Kelly, Martin, and Daniel D. Garcia-Swartz. "The History of the Internet: The Missing Narratives." *SSRN Electronic Journal,* 2005.

Cohen, Fred. "Computer Viruses: Theory and Experiments." *Computer & Security,* vol. 6, 1987b, pp. 22–35.

Computer Fraud and Abuse Act of 1986: Report (to Accompany H.R. 4712) (Including Cost Estimate of the Congressional Budget Office). U.S. G.P.O., 1986b.

Edwards, Paul N. *The Closed World: Computers and the Politics of Discourse in Cold War America*. New York: ACLS History E-Book Project, 2005.

Elbe, Stefan. "Bodies as Battlefields: Toward the Medicalization of Insecurity." *International Political Sociology* 6, no. 3 (2012): 320–22.

Eisenberg, T., D. Gries, J. Hartmanis, D. Holcomb, M. S. Lynn, and T. Santoro. "The Cornell Commission: on Morris and the Worm." *Communications of the ACM* 32, no. 6 (January 1989b): 706–9.

Gallagher, Cornelius E. "The Computer and the Invasion of Privacy." *Proceedings of the Fifth SIGCPR Conference on Computer Personnel Research*, 1967.

Gersho, A. "Unclassified Summary: Involvement of NSA in the Development of the Data Encryption Standard." *IEEE Communications Society Magazine*, vol. 16, no. 6, 1978, pp. 53–55.

Hafner, Katie, and John Markoff. *Cyberpunk: Outlaws and Hackers on the Computer Frontier*. Simon & Schuster, 1995.

Helmreich, Stefan. "Flexible Infections: Computer Viruses, Human Bodies, Nation-States, Evolutionary Capitalism." *Science, Technology, & Human Values* 25, no. 4 (2000): 472–91.

Hill, Joshua and Nancy Marion, "Presidential Rhetoric on Cybercrime: links to terrorism?," *Criminal Justice Studies*, 29:2 (2016), 163–177.

Kaplan, Fred M. *Dark Territory: the Secret History of Cyber War*. New York: Simon & Schuster Paperbacks, 2017.

Kluth, Daniel. "The Computer, Virus Threat: A Survey of Current Criminal Statutes," Hamline Law Review 13, no. 2 (Spring 1990): 297–312.

de Leeuw, Karl. *The History of Information Security: a Comprehensive Handbook*. Amsterdam: Elsevier, 2007.

DeNardis, Laura. "A History of Internet Security." In *The History of Information Security*, 1st ed., 681–704. Elsevier Science, 2007.

Brenner, Susan. "History of Computer Crime." In *The History of Information Security*, 1st ed., 705–21. Elsevier Science, 2007b.

Marion, Camille. "Computer Viruses and the Law," Dickinson Law Review 93, no. 3 (Spring 1989): 625–642

Mello, Susan. "Administering the Antidote to Computer Viruses: A Comment on United States v. Morris," Rutgers Computer & Technology Law Journal 19, no. 1 (1993): 259–280.

Montgomery, John. *White-Collar Crime: Fourth Survey of Law*. Georgetown University Law Center, 1987.

Moschovitis, Christos J. P. *History of the Internet: a Chronology, 1843 to the Present*. Santa Barbara, CA: ABC-CLIO, 1999.

Pfaffenberger, Bryan. "The Social Meaning of the Personal Computer: Or, Why the Personal Computer Revolution Was No Revolution." *Anthropological Quarterly* 61, no. 1 (1988).

Rosenzweig, Roy. "Wizards, Bureaucrats, Warriors, and Hackers: Writing the History of the Internet." *The American Historical Review*, 1998.

Ross, Andrew. 1991. "Hacking away at the counterculture." In *Technoculture*, edited by Constance Penley and Andrew Ross, 107–34. Minneapolis: University of Minnesota Press.

Schultz, Eugene. "Internet Security: Risk Analysis, Strategies, and Firewalls." *Network Security*, vol. 1997, no. 7, 1997, p. 15.

Sterling, Bruce. "Science Fiction And The Internet." *Reading Science Fiction*, 2008, pp. 235–243.

Taddeo, Mariarosaria. "On the Risks of Relying on Analogies to Understand Cyber Conflicts." *Minds and Machines* 26, no. 4 (2016): 317–21.

Warner, Michael. "Cybersecurity: A Pre-History." *Intelligence and National Security*, vol. 27, no. 5, 2012, pp. 781–799.

"Wizards, Bureaucrats, Warriors, and Hackers: Writing the History of the Internet." *The American Historical Review*, 1998.

Wolff, Josephine. *You'll See This Message When It Is Too Late: the Legal and Economic Aftermath of Cybersecurity Breaches*. Cambridge: MIT Press, 2018.

Wolfe, Audra J. *Freedoms Laboratory: the Cold War Struggle for the Soul of Science*. Johns Hopkins University Press, 2018.

Zalloua, Zahi Anbra, and Bruce A. Magnusson. *Contagion: Health, Fear, Sovereignty*. Seattle and London: University of Washington Press, 2012.

CHAPTER 6

Network

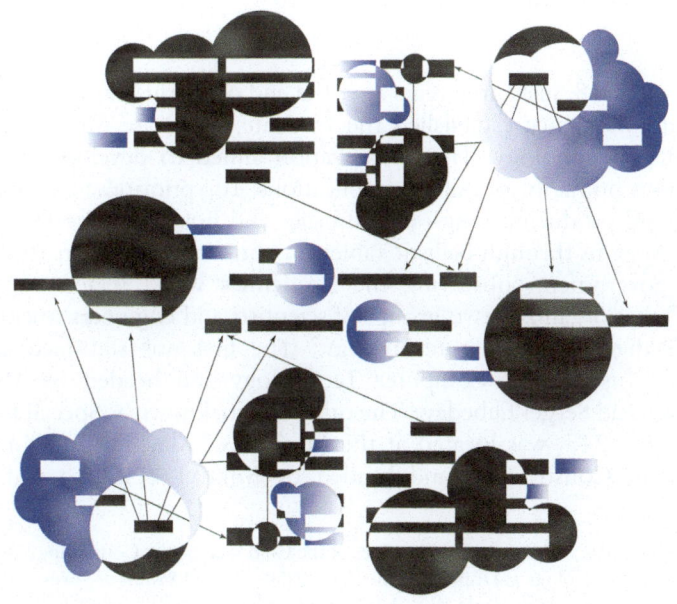

Internet #1 by Flora Weil

© The Author(s), under exclusive license to Springer Nature
Singapore Pte Ltd. 2025
R. Shemakov, *Centralized*,
https://doi.org/10.1007/978-981-96-2937-4_6

Abstract This chapter explores the development and control of the internet in the Soviet Union and post-Soviet Russia, highlighting its dual role as a tool for openness and state surveillance. Beginning with cybernetics and early Soviet computing projects, the narrative focuses on the rise of civilian internet networks like Relcom and Glasnet during the Glasnost years. Although these networks were crucial for bypassing censorship during the 1991 coup attempt, the following years saw escalating state intervention—particularly with the adoption of surveillance systems like SORM and stricter regulatory centralization—ultimately limiting internet freedoms and consolidating control under government authority. The chapter underscores the tension between the internet's potential for empowerment and its exploitation as an instrument of state power.

Keywords Cybernetics • OGAS Project • System of Operational-Investigatory Measures (SORM-2) • Relcom network • Glasnost

In June of 1948, just three years after the end of World War II, the Soviet Academy of Science established the Institute of Precise Mechanics and Computer Technology. This organization aimed to develop computer technology primarily for military applications. Top priorities included simulating and producing long-range missiles and bolstering the U.S.S.R.'s defense systems through ballistic tables for anti-aircraft fire.[1] In 1950, the Soviet government, observing the Academy's work, issued a "secret decree" that organized two groups of scientists and engineers to enhance Russia's digital computer technology.[2] The first was stationed at the Academy Institute of Computer Technology and headed by Mikhail Lavrentev and Sergei Lebedev.[3] The other group, known as Special Design Bureau No. 245, was located at the Ministry of Machine Building and Instrument Construction and headed by Mikhail Lesechko and Iurii

---

[1] Slava Gerovitch, "Mathematical Machines of the Cold War: Soviet Computing, American Cybernetics and Ideological Disputes in the Early 1950s." *Social Studies of Science* 31, no. 2, Special Issue: Science in the Cold War (April 2001): 265.

[2] Gerovitch, "Mathematical Machines of the Cold War," 265.

[3] Lavrentev was an "expert in mathematical modeling of explosions." He called upon the Soviet Academy of Sciences to create an institute dedicated to "mathematics and computer technology" in the military sphere. Lebedev was an engineer who also served as Director of the Institute of Electrical Engineering in Kyiv. Gerovitch, "Mathematical Machines of the Cold War," 265–6.

Bazilevskii. The Soviet Union proposed three separate computer systems for "air defense … missile defense … space surveillance" that would operate through individual computer networks.[4]

The following decade saw rapid advancements in Soviet computing technology. In 1951, the MESM "Small Electronic Calculating Machine" pioneered in Kyiv as "the first operating stored-program computer in continental Europe."[5] The M-I "Automatic Computing Machine" and the M-2, used for calculations for missile design, soon followed. The Soviet Union worked to optimize technology for nuclear physics and missile defense calculations, including the specialized STRELA computer (1953) and BESM "Large Electronic Calculating Machine" (1955). These developments remained under wraps until October 1955 when the U.S.S.R. publicized its progress to Europe—and the world—at the Conference of Electronic Digital Computers and Information Processing in Germany.

After Joseph Stalin's death in 1953, his successor Nikita Khrushchev pledged personal and financial support to the Institute of Precise Mechanics and Computer Technology, as well as to Lavrentev's projects.[6] During this period, Soviet scientists began to recognize the potential of cybernetics—a field encompassing the study of control and communication in animals, humans, and machines, closely associated with the development of computer systems and programs. Though initially dismissed due to its association with Western science and American origins, cybernetics gradually gained acceptance in the Soviet Union. Some scientists also began to question the government's restrictions on non-military research, which stemmed from ideological anxieties about Western influence.[7]

---

[4] Slava Gerovitch, "InterNyet: Why the Soviet Union Did Not Build a Nationwide Computer Network," *History and Technology* 24, no. 4 (December 2008): 338.

[5] Gerovitch, "Mathematical Machines of the Cold War," 265.

[6] Gerovitch, "Mathematical Machines of the Cold War," 267.

[7] Norbert Wiener's Cybernetics, a work which applied mathematical principles to "human-machine analogies … control and feedback mechanisms," was highly influential during this period. Juha Kukkola, "Digital Soviet Union: The Russian National Segment of the Internet as a Closed National Network Shaped by Strategic Cultural Ideas." Academic Dissertation presented with the permission of the Research Council of National Defence University, for public criticism for the degree of Doctor of Military Sciences, Santahamina, Helsinki, Finnish National Defence University, 2020. Soviet professor and scientist Arnost Kolman describes a "broad campaign against cybernetics" prior to the Soviet Union recognizing the potential benefits of such technology. E.S. and Arnost Kolman, "The Adventure of Cybernetics in the Soviet Union." Minerva 16, no. 3 (Autumn 1978): 422.

Arnost Kolman, a professor at the Moscow Institute of Mathematics and Mechanics and a member of the State Scientific Council of the Soviet Union, voiced these concerns. In 1958, speaking at a convention organized by the Soviet Academy of Sciences, Kolman warned that "the Soviet Union was already a full decade behind the United States in this field" and that Soviet computer production "was on a low level" by comparison.[8] He highlighted the government's reluctance to support civilian technology development, contrasting it with significant investments in military computing projects. At the time, only one facility—the Computation Centre of the Soviet Academy of Sciences—was dedicated to civilian computing, while military projects like the high-speed M-40 computer introduced by the Institute of Precise Mechanics and Computer Technology in 1958 received substantial funding.

In contrast to the military-focused M-40, the M-20 "general purpose" computer, completed just months later, operated at half the capacity and received far less attention.[9] Kolman accused the government of obstructing permits for scientists to study emerging computer technology and criticized the Communist Party's practice of censoring scientific papers. The Party often modified or deleted any information traceable to "anti-Soviet" origins, and a single veto could block a paper from publication.[10] Kolman asserted that scientific research related to the military was far more likely to receive governmental support, hindering the advancement of civilian technology and broader scientific progress.

Arnost Kolman's warnings came during a period of heightened censorship in the Soviet Union, a time when the nation's focus on computer technology was heavily centered on defense applications. Over the next decade, Soviet scientists began to explore how computers could be utilized more broadly within a communist framework. The 1961 Cybernetics Council of the Soviet Academy of Sciences advocated for the application of "computer and cybernetic models in a wide range of fields."[11] This proposal received approval from the Twenty-Second Congress of the Communist Party held the same year. It adopted a plan to establish a

---

[8] E.S. Kolman, "The Adventure of Cybernetics," 423.
[9] Gerovitch, "Mathematical Machines of the Cold War," 265–269.
[10] E.S. and Kolman. "The Adventure of Cybernetics," 423.
[11] Gerovitch, "InterNyet," 335.

"technical basis of communism" through programs for the "planning and management" of a communist economy.[12] By 1967, 500 cybernetic institutions operated under the auspices of the Cybernetics Council, with about half dedicated to economic research and applications.[13]

A leading figure in this movement was Viktor Glushkov, director of the Kyiv Institute of Cybernetics. In 1963, Glushkov outlined an ambitious plan for a Soviet computer network. He envisioned 100–200 large computer centers located in cities—referred to as "regional nodes"—and around 20,000 smaller centers positioned in government buildings and other organizations.[14] However, Glushkov's plan was expensive, controversial, and required unprecedented cooperation between the central government and local agencies. Additionally, the Soviet Union was undergoing political changes. In October 1964, Leonid Brezhnev replaced Nikita Khrushchev as the leader of the Communist Party, while Aleksei Kosygin became the Prime Minister. The new administration viewed Glushkov's plan for "automated economic management" as a threat to the existing balance of power. They sought to modify his proposals to suit their own objectives, which included rejecting his idea of a central data bank.[15] As a result, the Party sidelined Glushkov's model but continued to support the use of economic computer management systems in a more controlled manner.

Undeterred, Glushkov became involved in a second project: the All-State Automated System for the Collection and Processing of Information for the Accounting, Planning, and Governance of the National Economy, abbreviated in Russian as OGAS. The Twenty-fourth Party Congress approved the OGAS program in 1971. Glushkov envisioned a computer system that would create a digital hierarchy for all institutions involved in the Soviet economy, including the government, ministries, state committees, regional centers, and others. The system would automate their economic data by "balancing resources against end uses" and performing rapid calculations.[16] Importantly, OGAS was not meant to influence how the economy functioned fundamentally; rather, it was designed to organize and manage information more efficiently.

[12] Gerovitch, "InterNyet," 335.
[13] Gerovitch, "InterNyet," 337–338.
[14] Gerovitch, "InterNyet," 341.
[15] Gerovitch, "InterNyet," 341.
[16] William J. Conyngham, "Technology and Decision Making: Some Aspects of the Development of OGAS," *Slavic Review* 39, no. 3 (September 1980): 429.

Despite its potential, OGAS faced significant obstacles in implementation. Soviet leaders disagreed over the advantages of OGAS and many questioned its feasibility. The government attempted to centralize economic management through reforms of national ministries, granting them increased power to oversee regional economic development.[17] This move was intended to prepare the ministries for integration into OGAS.[18] However, instead of collaborating under the new system, the ministries exploited the reforms to "strengthen ... control over sensitive information."[19] They developed individualized hardware and software systems that were incompatible with one another, making broader collaboration impossible. As a result, any "branch networks" that they created were unsustainable.[20]

Recognizing these challenges, the Communist Party withdrew its initial support for OGAS and scaled back the plan to focus on individualized computer centers rather than a national network. In both 1976 and 1981, the Party revisited proposals for OGAS, but these efforts also failed to progress beyond the ministry level. The persistent inability to implement a unified Soviet internet meant that Glushkov's vision of a nationwide computer network never came to fruition.[21]

After the death of Leonid Brezhnev in 1982, the Soviet Union underwent a period of political transition that eventually led to the rise of Mikhail Gorbachev as the General Secretary of the Communist Party in 1985. Gorbachev introduced a series of reforms known as Perestroika (restructuring) and Glasnost (openness), which significantly impacted the country's political systems and the role of information technology.

Despite the earlier failure to implement a unified national computer network like OGAS, the development of the internet and digital communication continued to progress, slowly becoming a source of information and a means for widespread communication. Under Gorbachev's Glasnost policy, restrictions on media were relaxed, offering greater freedom to both print and digital outlets. This represented a significant departure from the stringent censorship policies of the mid-twentieth century. The government reduced the powers of *Glavlit*, the agency responsible for

---

[17] Gerovitch, "InterNyet," 346.
[18] Conyngham, "Technology and Decision Making," 427.
[19] Gerovitch, "InterNyet," 346.
[20] Gerovitch, "InterNyet," 346.
[21] Gerovitch, "InterNyet," 346.

monitoring and censoring publications, allowing for increased access to previously suppressed information.[22]

Gorbachev and those who shared his political vision "tolerated increased access to previously suppressed information [among] the masses" in the interest of guiding the Soviet Union into the modern "media ecosystem."[23] In line with these reforms, the Soviet government enacted the Law of the Press and Other Mass Information Media in 1990—commonly referred to as the Soviet Mass Media Law. This legislation guaranteed freedom of the press, marking a substantial change from the precedents set during the Cold War. It granted individual citizens the right to "establish a press organ" and defined the consequences for interfering with journalistic freedom.[24]

However, the liberalization of media and information also intensified political tensions within the Soviet leadership. By early 1991, less than a year before the eventual dissolution of the Soviet Union, a power struggle emerged between Gorbachev and Boris Yeltsin. Gorbachev had appointed Yeltsin as the head of the Moscow Communist Party Committee in 1985, but Yeltsin soon began to build his own political base. He criticized the Communist Party Congress and the existing regime, advocating for more radical reforms. In response, Gorbachev attempted to block Yeltsin from gaining further influence.[25]

In August 1991, a coup was launched by hardline members of the Communist Party and government officials who opposed Gorbachev's policies, including Glasnost and the new media freedoms. The group, calling themselves the State Committee of the State of Emergency, sought to reverse the liberalization policies. They advocated for renewed censorship and banned the majority of Moscow's newspapers, permitting only nine "state controlled" papers to remain active.[26] Despite his previous criticisms

---

[22] Joshua Baker, "Russian Internet Censorship and Its Future Perspectives in Comparative Context." Submitted to the Eberly College of Arts and Sciences at West Virginia University in partial fulfillment of the requirements for the degree of Master of Arts in History, West Virginia University, 2011. The Research Repository at WVU, 5.

[23] Julien Nocetti, "Contest and Conquest: Russia and Global Internet Governance." *International Affairs* 91, no. 1 (2015): 129.

[24] Baker, "Russian Internet Censorship," 7.

[25] Marc Zlotnik, "Yeltsin and Gorbachev," *Journal of Cold War Studies* 5, no. 2 (Winter 2003): 132.

[26] Baker, "Russian Internet Censorship," 8.

of Gorbachev, Yeltsin condemned the coup, positioning himself as a defender of democratic reforms.

Amid the coup's crackdown on traditional media and communications, an alternative means of disseminating information emerged through a digital network known as Relcom/Demos.[27] The origins of the Relcom network dated back to discarded economic internet projects of the 1960s.[28] By 1991, Relcom/Demos had established nodes across large parts of the Soviet Union, although it remained a private enterprise primarily used for social communication.

During the crisis, "programmers and scientists ... recognized that the 'unofficial' net allowed them to bypass the formal bureaucratic hierarchy."[29] Many took it upon themselves to "[email] Yeltsin's defiant declaration, rejecting the legitimacy of the coup committee to Russia's outlying regions and abroad."[30] Journalists, too, published reports through Relcom/Demos, and the network became "an active channel of communication" between Moscow and those across the nation who opposed the coup.[31]

The international response to these digital communications was significant. Messages of support and inquiries flooded in from abroad, to the extent that the network became overloaded. The programmers managing Relcom/Demos had to "plead with Westerners" to limit their messages to prevent the system from collapsing under the increased traffic.[32] The 1991 coup attempt thus marked the public debut of Relcom/Demos as a vital tool for information exchange, highlighting the emerging role of the internet as a platform for political discourse and resistance in the Soviet Union.[33]

Relcom/Demos was not the only network involved in the coup. Russian users also took to Glasnet—an internet service provider (ISP) less than a

[27] Zlotnik, "Yeltsin and Gorbachev," 151. Rafal Rohozinski, "How the Internet Did Not Transform Russia," *Current History* 99, no. 639 (October 2000): 334.

[28] Rohozinski, "How the Internet Did Not Transform Russia," 337.

[29] Rohozinski, "How the Internet Did Not Transform Russia," 337.

[30] As Rafal Rohozinski elaborates, the coup coalition, consisting of the vice-president, KGB chairman, and Ministers of the Defense and the Interior, chose to take action in August when Gorbachev and other governmental figures were "absent from Moscow." Rafal Rohozinski, "Mapping Russian Cyberspace: Perspectives on Democracy and the Net. UNRISD Discussion Paper No. 115." Discussion Paper (Geneva, Switzerland: United Nations Research Institute for Social Development, October 1999), introduction.

[31] Rohozinski, "How the Internet Did Not Transform Russia," 334.

[32] Rohozinski, "Mapping Russian Cyberspace," introduction.

[33] Rohozinski, "How the Internet Did Not Transform Russia," 335.

year old in 1991—to share information with the "breathless outside world."[34] Relcom and Glasnet played distinct roles in communication efforts during the coup. Glasnet, "one of the first Russian computer networks with a direct connection to the Internet," acted as one of several "paraskeletal networks" that defied the coup's censorship efforts.[35]

The network was best known among an elite class of Moscow intellectuals and researchers, along with some foreigners and a "new class of rich Russians."[36] By contrast, Relcom, dominated by programmers, was the "main internal link" between Moscow and the rest of Russia.[37] As a result, it "facilitated widespread resistance among non-institutionalized lines."[38] Thus, the use of Relcom proved more influential for the evolution of the internet within Russia, while Glasnet served as the West's introduction to the Russian internet.[39] While the extent to which Relcom and Glasnet impacted the coup remains a subject of debate, the coup was defeated in short order, while Glasnost and the Media Law remained in effect.[40] Nonetheless, the situation had damaged Gorbachev's political reputation, and Yeltsin carried the June 12 presidential election with 57 percent of the vote.[41]

---

[34] Specter, "Russians' Newest Space Adventure: Cyberspace," 1994.

[35] Michael Specter, "Russians' Newest Space Adventure: Cyberspace," *New York Times*, March 9, 1994, Times Machine; Rohozinski, "Mapping Russian Cyberspace," 2.

[36] Rohozinski, "Mapping Russian Cyberspace," iv.

[37] Rohozinski, "Mapping Russian Cyberspace," 2.

[38] Rohozinski, "Mapping Russian Cyberspace," 9.

[39] Relcom never existed as a "unified whole." Relcom Nodes refer to nodes used by "private companies" to communicate with the primary Relcom node based in Moscow. Rohozinski, "Mapping Russian Cyberspace," 9.

[40] Rafal Rohozinski argues against scholarship that points to the use of Relcom during the coup as evidence of Russian "social evolution" and "linear transformation" through the internet. In the decade after the coup, Russia's internet use has remained localized and has not reflected a desire to emulate or connect with democratic nations. Rohozinski further notes that the success of Relcom discredits the state: the Soviet Union failed to create "an open, Internet-type computer network," and this entity emerged only "outside [of] formal state control." Rohozinski, "How the Internet Did Not Transform Russia," 334–5.

[41] Zlotnik, "Yeltsin and Gorbachev," 153.

Relcom/Demos and Glasnet

Relcom, short for "Reliable Communications" in English translation, was the "first Soviet and Russian computer network" designed to facilitate email communications.[42] Initiated in the latter half of the 1980s, during a period of significant technological advancement and political change, Relcom was from the outset a commercial venture that charged users for every byte of data transmitted.[43] It began operating in 1990 and was programmed in tandem with "demos," the "first Russian Internet service provider."[44] Initially, Relcom functioned as a non-government enterprise, created by a group of Unix computer programmers aiming to improve communication between small groups dispersed across different locations.[45]

After the 1991 coup attempt, Relcom "gained a good reputation" in the eyes of the West and among like-minded "information agencies, newspaper editors, and magazine/journal publishers."[46] In late 1991, Relcom had more than 20,000 users across 120 towns and cities.[47] Several interrelated factors contributed to the rise of Relcom and its rapidly expanding user base. During the final years of the Soviet Union, commercial desktop computers became more "accessible" at the same time that mail and telephone communication services faced an "unprecedented shortage and unreliability."[48] These developments led to a shift in the demographics of Relcom subscribers as Russian intellectuals, including scientists, educators, businessmen, and journalists joined the network in large numbers.[49] Consequently, while computer programmers remained a significant portion of Relcom's users, the network evolved from a tool for professional

---

[42] "About Relcom - Documents - Relcom," accessed February 3, 2022; Rohozinski, "Mapping Russian Cyberspace," 8.

[43] Rohozinski, "Mapping Russian Cyberspace," iv.

[44] "About Relcom - Documents - Relcom," accessed February 3, 2022. After 1992, Relcom/Demos split into two separate companies. Rohozinski, "Mapping Russian Cyberspace," 9.

[45] Alexander E. Voiskounsky, "The Relcom Network: An Investigation of Its Users," *Journal of Computer-Mediated Communication* 2, no. 4 (June 23, 2006), https://doi.org/10.1111/j.1083-6101.1997.tb00198.x.

[46] Voiskounsky, "The Relcom Network."

[47] Rohozinski, "Mapping Russian Cyberspace," 8.

[48] Voiskounsky, "The Relcom Network."

[49] Voiskounsky, "The Relcom Network."

communication among programmers to a broader platform serving various sectors of society.[50]

As Relcom and Glasnet expanded, Yeltsin took steps toward promoting freedom of the press. In December 1992, Yeltsin enacted a second Media Law, building upon the earlier 1990 Mass Media Law. These laws marked critical milestones in Russian media history, allowing both domestic and international audiences access to information that had previously been suppressed during the Soviet era. However, Yeltsin tempered these advancements by including provisions that permitted censorship for security reasons or to protect against the dissemination of material deemed distasteful. This caveat introduced a potential legal loophole, necessitating state monitoring of the media to determine suitability of content for public consumption.[51]

In the same year, the government passed the 1992 Database Law, which focused on internet security rather than direct media censorship. This law provided safeguards for software designers and offered limited privacy protection for digital communications. Simultaneously, it established a "registration mechanism" to help the state monitor technological progress and internet usage, reflecting the government's interest in maintaining oversight of the rapidly developing digital landscape.[52]

Amid a constitutional crisis in 1993, Yeltsin's commitment to media freedom was tested. Facing opposition from the parliament, he dissolved the legislative body, prompting widespread media outrage. In response to critical press coverage, Yeltsin suspended several newspapers—a move that contravened the provisions of the Media Law. According to the law, the dissolution of any media outlet required prior warning and a court decision, powers vested solely in the judicial branch.[53] Despite this conflict, Yeltsin eventually consolidated his position, overcoming the challenge posed by his vice-president, Alexander Rutskoi, whom the disbanded parliament had attempted to install as president. Following his reinstatement, a new Russian Constitution was adopted, guaranteeing rights to free speech and unrestricted freedom of the media but prohibiting "propaganda."[54] This indicated that while freedom of the press was

---

[50] Voiskounsky, "The Relcom Network."
[51] Baker, "Russian Internet Censorship," 8–9.
[52] Alexander, "The Internet and Democratization," 616.
[53] Baker, "Russian Internet Censorship," 9.
[54] Baker, "Russian Internet Censorship," 14–15.

enshrined, the state retained the authority to oversee media communications.

In his later years in office, Yeltsin's policies reflected a shift toward tighter control over information, as the internet began to be viewed as an agent of Westernization and a potential threat to national sovereignty.[55] At the same time, the United States took notice of "the Russian-language Telkom network" and characterized it as a symptom of Russia's "growing electronic addiction."[56] A 1994 *New York Times* article highlighted the surge in internet usage, noting that "tens of thousands of people, from scientists and bankers to truck manufacturers and astrologers," were tapping into new internet services.[57] Despite limited access to high-speed computers—"the fruits of Russian military technology never trickled down to the hacker," the article noted cynically.[58] But Relcom provided 200,000 subscribers inexpensive access to a world of instant communication.

In 1994, the Russian government issued the Roskominform Statute, establishing a "hybrid executive-legislative body" with broad authority over the Russian media.[59] The responsibilities held by the Roskominform included establishing "national priorities," drafting new laws, and cooperating with "international bodies."[60] This move signaled an increasing governmental interest in regulating information flow. The following year, the 1995 Law on Informational Investigations represented a step toward overt state intervention in private communication. This legislation authorized the Federal Security Service (FSB)—the successor to the KGB—to monitor citizens' private communications, including internet activity. Additionally, President Yeltsin decreed a ban on internet encryption algorithms not certified by the Federal Agency for Government Communications and Information, akin to the U.S. National Security Agency.[61]

---

[55] Nocetti, "Contest and Conquest," 114.

[56] The *New York Times* article refers to the network Relcom as "Relkom." The spelling "Relcom" is more common. Specter, "Russians' Newest Space Adventure: Cyberspace," 1994.

[57] Specter, "Russians' Newest Space Adventure: Cyberspace," 1994.

[58] Specter, "Russians' Newest Space Adventure: Cyberspace," 1994.

[59] Alexander, "The Internet and Democratization," 614–615.

[60] Alexander, "The Internet and Democratization," 614.

[61] Rohozinski, "How the Internet Did Not Transform Russia," 338.

In the same vein, Russia implemented the "System of Operational-Investigatory Measures (SORM)" in 1995.[62] Under SORM, all internet service providers (ISPs) were required to install hardware that allowed the FSB to monitor telecommunications. This meant that "phone calls, email traffic, and web browsing activity" were no longer protected as personal information.[63] Several years later, SORM-2 expanded the FSB's capabilities by permitting broader "monitoring of internet traffic" without the need for warrants.[64]

Email communications became a particular point of concern for the Russian government during the implementation of SORM. The *New York Times* article that publicized the rise of Relcom also described a shift in Russia from "unreliable communications services to a growing electronic mail network."[65] Anatoly A. Voronov, the director of Glasnet, had a simple explanation for the takeoff of email services: "email succeeds here in part because everything [else] fails so badly."[66] Voronov explained that ineffective networks for physical mail encouraged Russian citizens to put their faith in new technology. Email eradicated many of the issues with traditional communication by post. Email offered a faster, cheaper alternative, allowing users to send "documents of virtually unlimited length" instantaneously.[67]

Two years later, Voronov was quoted in a second *New York Times* article discussing the American influence on global internet technology. In contrast to his stance in 1994, Voronov adopted a more critical perspective. He described the World Wide Web as "the ultimate act of intellectual colonialism," referring to the dominance of American software and the necessity of English proficiency to operate it.[68] Voronov pointed out that a Russian speaker could easily find an English translation of Dostoevsky's

[62] Nathalie Maréchal, "Networked Authoritarianism and the Geopolitics of Information: Understanding Russian Internet Policy." "Post-Snowden Internet Policy," *Media and Communication*, 5, no. 1 (March 22, 2017): 33.

[63] Maréchal, "Networked Authoritarianism," 33.

[64] Jaclyn A. Kerr, Ph.D. "The Russian Model of Internet Control and Its Significance." Lawrence Livermore National Laboratory under auspices of U.S. Department of Energy, December 21, 2018, 2.

[65] Specter, "Russians' Newest Space Adventure: Cyberspace," 1994.

[66] Anatoly A. Voronov, quoted in Specter, "Russians' Newest Space Adventure."

[67] David A. Allie, "The Internet and Research: Explanation and Resources," *The Journal of Mind and Behavior* 16, no. 4 (Autumn 1995): 340.

[68] Anatoly A. Voronov, quoted in Specter, "Computer Speak; World, Wide, Web: 3 English Words," 1996.

works online but would struggle to acquire them in the original Russian. "This just makes the world into new sorts of haves and have nots," he remarked.[69] Despite these concerns, the Russian public continued to embrace the internet, and as networks like Relcom grew, the implications of SORM's surveillance capabilities became increasingly significant.

The introduction of SORM-2 is difficult to date precisely. The FSB acknowledged the existence of SORM-2 draft legislation in mid-1998, long before it was "signed and published in open media."[70] Russian ISPs felt the effects in 1999 when those without SORM systems were threatened with the loss of their operating licenses, even though the FSB did not gain "presidential assent" to implement SORM-2 until 2000.[71] SORM-2 represented a substantial intrusion into internet privacy. It mandated the inclusion of "surveillance devices" and "high speed links to the Federal Security Service," allowing the agency to access internet communications without first obtaining a court warrant.[72] It also forced ISPs to "route their … data through FSB computers," a process that simplified government surveillance.[73]

Service providers that resisted implementing SORM-2 faced severe consequences, including being disconnected from the network.[74] For example, such a case occurred when Bayard-Slavia threatened to sue the FSB for seeking to collect users' passwords. In 1999, Russia had 360 ISPs in total, 90 percent of which were "small sub providers."[75] By 2000, Relcom and Demos had become the largest internet service providers in Russia. Relcom alone had about 10,000 users in Moscow and operated around 150 regional hubs, each serving between 500 to 1000 subscribers.[76] Having become "entirely government-owned," Relcom dominated

---

[69] Voronov, quoted in Specter, "Computer Speak; World, Wide, Web."

[70] David Banisar and Simon Davies, "Global Trends in Privacy Protection: An International Survey of Privacy, Data Protection, and Surveillance Laws and Developments, 18 J. Marshall J. Computer & Info. L. 1 (1999)," *The John Marshall Journal of Information Technology & Privacy Law* 18, no. 1 (Fall 1999): 85.

[71] Rohozinski, "How the Internet Did Not Transform Russia," 338.

[72] Banisar and Davies, "Global Trends in Privacy Protection," 85.

[73] Alexander, "The Internet and Democratization," 616.

[74] Alexander, "The Internet and Democratization," 616.

[75] Alexander, "The Internet and Democratization," 616.

[76] Marcus Alexander, "The Internet and Democratization: The Development of Russian Internet Policy." *Demokratizatsiya: The Journal of Post-Soviet Democratization* (October 10, 2001): 612.

the market.[77] Within the next two years, five operators (including Relcom) controlled 84 percent of all ISP services in Russia.[78] The high cost of the required SORM-2 hardware made it challenging for smaller providers to comply with the FSB's demands, leading to further consolidation in the industry.

SORM-2 did not unfold exactly as the FSB had envisioned. Within Russia's network community, it gained a reputation for being "unenforceable and impractical," partly due to the sheer volume of data generated by increasing internet traffic.[79] Early efforts to reform SORM-2 after 1999 highlighted the risks such legislation posed to internet freedoms, especially among ISPs still operating outside direct government control. One proposed reform required the FSB to obtain a court warrant before accessing information from internet records—a provision absent from the original legislation. However, this reform was undermined by subsequent actions.

One of Vladimir Putin's early decisions upon becoming president in 2000 was to expand access to SORM data beyond the FSB. He authorized other organizations, including tax authorities and the Presidential Security Service, to utilize SORM-collected information, effectively nullifying the requirement for judicial oversight. Additionally, while the reform stipulated that surveillance of the actual content of communications required a warrant, it still allowed for the collection of metadata—information about the origin and destination of digital communications. Even without access to the specific content, the FSB could gather significant information through this loophole.[80]

The 1991 coup attempt in the Soviet Union catalyzed the emergence of the internet as a crucial tool for open communication, with networks like Relcom disseminating information during the crisis and bypassing government censorship. This highlighted the internet's potential to empower citizens and facilitate free exchange of ideas. Recognizing this, the internet became considerably more centralized. Financially, the substantial infrastructure requirements placed heavy burdens on independent service providers. Those with scale and financing rose above the rest. On the regulatory side, the government introduced laws that increased

[77] Alexander, "The Internet and Democratization," 612.
[78] Alexander, "The Internet and Democratization," 612.
[79] Rohozinski, "How the Internet Did Not Transform Russia," 338.
[80] Maréchal, "Networked Authoritarianism," 33.

oversight and control over digital communications, such as requiring ISPs to install FSB monitoring equipment and permitting surveillance without warrants. These regulatory demands made it difficult for smaller ISPs to operate independently, effectively centralizing the internet infrastructure under government control. Thus, while the coup spurred the internet's rise as a tool for openness, the government's deliberate financial and regulatory centralization ultimately diminished that openness by enhancing control over all digital communications.

BIBLIOGRAPHY

E.S. and Arnost Kolman. "The Adventure of Cybernetics in the Soviet Union." *Minerva* 16, no. 3 (Autumn 1978): 422.

"Information Security Doctrine of The Russian Federation, Approved by President of the Russian Federation Vladimir Putin on September 9, 2000." September 9, 2000, 2.

Gerovitch, Slava. "Mathematical Machines of the Cold War: Soviet Computing, American Cybernetics and Ideological Disputes in the Early 1950s." *Social Studies of Science* 31, no. 2 (April 2001): 265.

———. "InterNyet: Why the Soviet Union Did Not Build a Nationwide Computer Network." *History and Technology* 24, no. 4 (December 2008): 338.

Conyngham, William J. "Technology and Decision Making: Some Aspects of the Development of OGAS." *Slavic Review* 39, no. 3 (September 1980): 429.

Nocetti, Julien. "Contest and Conquest: Russia and Global Internet Governance." *International Affairs* 91, no. 1 (2015): 129.

Zlotnik, Marc. "Yeltsin and Gorbachev." *Journal of Cold War Studies* 5, no. 2 (Winter 2003): 132.

Specter, Michael. "Russians' Newest Space Adventure: Cyberspace." *New York Times*, March 9, 1994. TimesMachine.

Rohozinski, Rafal. "Mapping Russian Cyberspace," 2. (Note: This entry is incomplete as provided; consider combining or citing fully if referencing both sources separately.)

Voiskounsky, Alexander E. "The Relcom Network: An Investigation of Its Users." *Journal of Computer-Mediated Communication* 2, no. 4 (June 23, 2006). https://doi.org/10.1111/j.1083-6101.1997.tb00198.x.

Specter, Michael. "Computer Speak; World, Wide, Web: 3 English Words." *New York Times*, April 14, 1996, sec. 4. TimesMachine.

Maréchal, Nathalie. "Networked Authoritarianism and the Geopolitics of Information: Understanding Russian Internet Policy." In "Post-Snowden Internet Policy." *Media and Communication* 5, no. 1 (March 22, 2017): 33.

Kerr, Jaclyn A., Ph.D. "The Russian Model of Internet Control and Its Significance." Lawrence Livermore National Laboratory, under the auspices of the U.S. Department of Energy, December 21, 2018, 2.

Allie, David A. "The Internet and Research: Explanation and Resources." *The Journal of Mind and Behavior* 16, no. 4 (Autumn 1995): 340.

Voronov, Anatoly A. Quoted in Michael Specter, "Computer Speak; World, Wide, Web: 3 English Words." *New York Times*, April 14, 1996, sec. 4. TimesMachine.

Banisar, David, and Simon Davies. "Global Trends in Privacy Protection: An International Survey of Privacy, Data Protection, and Surveillance Laws and Developments, 18 J. Marshall J. Computer & Info. L. 1 (1999)." *The John Marshall Journal of Information Technology & Privacy Law* 18, no. 1 (Fall 1999): 85.

Alexander, Marcus. "The Internet and Democratization: The Development of Russian Internet Policy." *Demokratizatsiya: The Journal of Post-Soviet Democratization* (October 10, 2001): 612.

CHAPTER 7

Edge

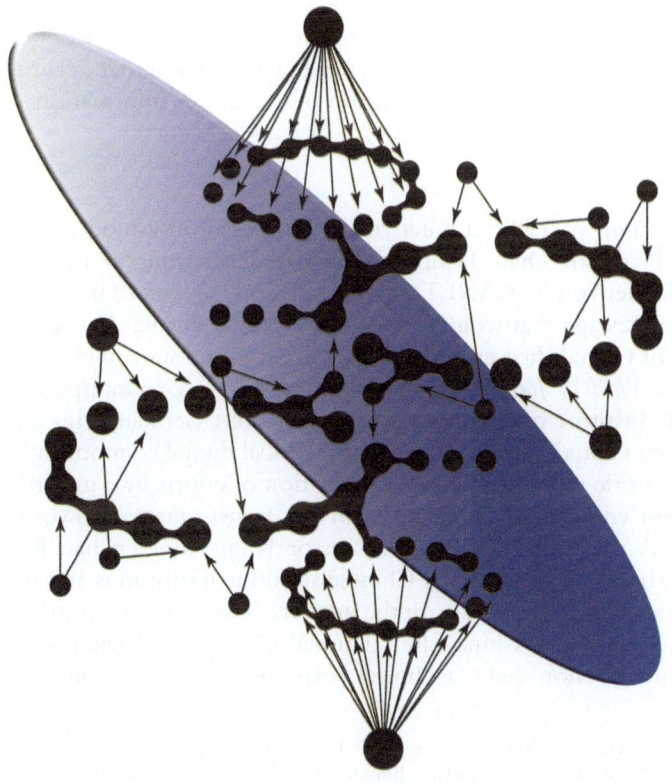

Internet #2 by Flora Weil

© The Author(s), under exclusive license to Springer Nature
Singapore Pte Ltd. 2025
R. Shemakov, *Centralized*,
https://doi.org/10.1007/978-981-96-2937-4_7

Abstract This chapter traces the emergence of the internet in China, starting with the country's first email in 1987 and the subsequent efforts to establish a global digital presence. It highlights the role of American technology companies, reforms under Deng Xiaoping, and agreements with the United States in building China's earliest internet infrastructure. While the internet enabled significant economic and technological growth, it also prompted the Chinese government to implement strict content regulations to maintain political control. By exploring legislative milestones and partnerships with both domestic and foreign entities, the chapter underscores the tension between technological innovation and centralized governance.

Keywords Cyber sovereignty • Sino-American Technology Cooperation • Provisional Regulations on Networking (1996) • Internet Security Regulations (1997) • Safety Protection of Computer Information Systems (SPCIS)

In the autumn of 1987, a quiet revolution began in a modest office in Beijing. Professor Qian Tianbai, a dedicated academic at the Chinese Academic Network's (CANET) internet project, sat before his computer, crafting a message that would bridge a vast digital divide.[1] On September 20, he sent China's first email, a simple yet profound statement: *"Crossing the Great Wall to Join the World."* Addressed to a counterpart at the Karlsruhe Institute of Technology in former West Germany, this message symbolized China's earnest step into the global digital community.

This historic moment was the culmination of efforts by a group of scientists and engineers who believed in the transformative power of the internet. A year prior, in 1987, Professor Wang Yungfen had founded CANET, bringing together 28 Chinese scientific institutions and inviting foreign experts to collaborate on the project.[2] The network's primary mission was to establish China's foundational internet infrastructure, a task that required not only technical expertise but also international

---

[1] Zorn, Werner. Issue brief. China's CSNET Connection 1987—Origin of the China Academic Network CANET. Potsdam, Brandenburg: Hasso-Plattner-Institute at Potsdam University/KIT—Karlsruhe Institute of Technology, 2012.

[2] Ibid.

cooperation. Members of CANET worked closely with engineers from global companies like Siemens of Germany. These collaborations were crucial in setting up the base infrastructure needed for China to connect with the rest of the world.

The momentum continued in 1988 when Tsinghua University's campus network linked up with the University of British Columbia in Canada through the X.25 network. Then, in 1990, Professor Qian officially registered China's domain name ".CN" with the Defense Data Network— Network Information Center (DDN-NIC), the original international internet regulator.[3] This act officially marked China's presence on the global internet stage. Most of these pioneering efforts unfolded within the campuses of Peking University and Tsinghua University, where scholars and students eagerly explored internet's possibilities.[4] However, despite these advancements, China remained only partially connected to the global network. The U.S. government, wary of sharing valuable scientific and technological information with socialist nations, had imposed restrictions that limited China's access to the internet.

Chinese scientists and officials sought to overcome these restrictions. Their efforts bore fruit at the 1993 INET Conference, where China finally secured the support of participating nations to gain full internet access. The following year, in 1994, during the Sino-American Federation of Scientific and Technological Cooperation meeting in Washington, D.C., Chinese and American scientists convened to discuss potential collaborations. Representing China was Hu Qihuan, the vice-president of the Chinese Academy of Sciences. Hu was instrumental in founding the China Internet Network Information Center and served as the president of China's Internet Society (ISC).

At the conference, Hu appealed on behalf of the Chinese government for China's linkage to the National Science Foundation (NSF) network in the United States.[5] His appeal was ultimately accepted, a decision that

---

[3] CERNET. "Evolution of Internet in China." China Education and Research Network. China Education and Research Network, January 1, 2001. http://www.edu.cn/introduction_1378/20060323/t20060323_4285.shtml.

[4] Ibid.

[5] Ibid.

would have far-reaching implications for China's technological advancement. That same year, the Sino-American Internet Agreement was signed. Under this agreement, China Telecom opened two 64k dedicated circuits in Beijing and Shanghai through the Sprint telecommunications company in the United States. This development officially marked the commencement of work on China's internet, colloquially known as "Chinanet."

While these technological strides were being made, China was also undergoing profound transformations in its science and technology policies and legal structure. Before these reforms, China had modeled its system after the Soviet Union, with a highly centralized approach to research and development. Public research institutes conducted most of the scientific research under the directives of the central government, while universities focused solely on educating engineers and innovators. This system, while effective in some respects, stifled innovation and limited the potential for private enterprise.

In the late 1970s, under the leadership of Deng Xiaoping, China began to break away from the Soviet model. The country embarked on a series of reforms aimed at motivating research institutions, universities, and private enterprises to collaborate on fundamental technological breakthroughs.[6] These reforms led to a significant increase in research and development (R&D) expenditure, which grew eightfold starting in 1987. Private enterprises began to play a more prominent role, contributing around 65 percent of development funding.[7]

The number of patent applications from Chinese innovators increased dramatically, and China's standing on global innovation rankings rose. However, the reforms also introduced new challenges. The centralized administrative structure of government agencies overseeing science and technology policy led to a lack of coordination. Additionally, the commercialization of the science and technology sector resulted in a brain drain from the public sector, as talented individuals were drawn to higher-paying positions in university-affiliated enterprises.

[6] Xiwei, Zhong, and Yang Xiangdong. "Science and Technology Policy Reform and Its Impact on China's National Innovation System." Technology in Society. Pergamon, May 25, 2007. https://www.sciencedirect.com/science/article/pii/S0160791X07000346.
[7] Ibid.

Parallel to the scientific reforms, China also overhauled its legal system to support the transition from a planned economy to a market economy. Over the decades, the National People's Congress passed numerous significant economic legislations, expanding the role of courts and lawyers.[8] By the early 1990s, the transition from a planned to a market economy entailed a reduction in the role of "individualized judgments of bureaucrats and an increase in the importance of universally applicable rules."[9]

Since the early days of internet development in China, Chinese entrepreneurs have taken full advantage of this new platform to connect with each other and with the world. Many of the well-known Chinese companies and websites today were born in the 1990s. For instance, Sina.com—the parent company of Weibo—was launched in 1996, NetEase in 1997, Tencent in 1998, Alibaba in 1999, and Baidu in 2000. These newly established companies knew the importance of internet development for China's overall economic modernization and advancement.[10]

These companies recognized the internet's potential to drive China's economic modernization and advancement. On December 30, 1999, 36 leading domestic internet companies proposed a collaboration between China's media and commercial entities. Their goal was to promote the development of the country's information and communication network in the coming century. Meanwhile, U.S. companies were paying close attention to China's transforming market and its vast consumer base. Companies like Cisco Systems, Yahoo, and Microsoft played significant roles in developing China's early internet infrastructure. Cisco and Juniper Networks

[8] Corne, Peter Howard. 2002. "Creation and Application of Law in the PRC." *The American Journal of Comparative Law* 50 (2): 369. https://doi.org/10.2307/840825.

[9] Clarke, Donald C. and Murrell, Peter and Whiting, Susan H., The Role of Law in China's Economic Development (2008). In Thomas Rawski and Loren Brandt (ed.), China's Great Economic Transformation (Cambridge University Press, 2008): 375–428. Available at SSRN: https://ssrn.com/abstract=878672 or https://doi.org/10.2139/ssrn.878672.

[10] CERNET. "Evolution of Internet in China." China Education and Research Network. China Education and Research Network, January 1, 2001. http://www.edu.cn/introduction_1378/20060323/t20060323_4285.shtml.

provided essential technology for internet routers and auxiliary hardware, while Yahoo and Microsoft offered software and internet services tailored to the Chinese network system.[11]

The involvement of American companies was not purely economic; it was also influenced by a strategic belief that integrating China into the global market would encourage political liberalization. Former President Bill Clinton, following China's accession to the World Trade Organization (WTO), states the following:

> [Chinese leaders] realize that if they open China's markets to global competition, they risk unleashing forces beyond their control … But they also know that, without competition from the outside, China will not be able to attract the investment necessary to build a modern, successful economy … We know how much the internet has changed America, and we are already an open society … Imagine how much it could change China.[12]

Other U.S. officials shared this perspective. Former Secretaries of State James A. Baker and Madeleine Albright argued that the internet would inevitably democratize the countries it entered.

However, while the internet's benefits—such as the free flow of information and the distribution of resources between enterprises and governmental mandates—were instrumental to China's economic success, they also posed challenges to the centralized governance. The Chinese government recognized that unchecked access to information could threaten social cohesion and political stability. As a result, they implemented stringent regulations on content filtering and censorship.

In 1994, the State Council promulgated the first Regulations for the Safety Protection of Computer Information Systems (SPCIS). This legislation focused on defining the hardware components of computer information systems and laid out the social intentions of the new technology for the "smooth fulfillment of socialist modernizations."[13] Although it did not immediately concern internet regulation and monitoring, it set the

---

[11] Lum, Thomas G., Internet development and information control in the People's Republic of China §. RL33167 (n.d.).

[12] Webster, Graham. "A Brief History of the Chinese Internet." Logic Magazine, March 14, 2021. https://logicmag.io/china/a-brief-history-of-the-chinese-internet/.

[13] "Laws of the People's Republic of China." AsianLII. AsianLII. Accessed January 29, 2022. http://www.asianlii.org/cn/legis/cen/laws/rfspocis719/.

stage for future policies. As internet usage grew, Beijing introduced a series of laws to govern and monitor online content. In 1996, China enacted the Provisional Regulations on the Management of International Networking of Computer Information Networks, which aimed to strengthen the administration of global computer networks and ensure healthy international cooperation.[14] This legislation required international information sources to be provided to and administered by the Ministry of Posts and Telecommunications, emphasizing control over the information entering the country.

Two months later, the Measures on the Regulation of Public Computer Networks and the Internet were introduced, marking the first regulation explicitly targeting internet censorship.[15] The preamble of this new legislation clearly defines the scope of the internet network in China as "China Public Computer Network," or "Chinanet," as the "interconnecting network built, operated, and managed by China's General Bureau of Posts and Telecommunications (GBPT)." Specifically, Article 4 also lists the organizations serving as "entry point units" for Chinanet as organizations that are legally established and "obey [the] laws and regulations of the country as well as requirements set up by the Ministry of Posts and Telecommunications (MPT)."[16]

Most notably, this law is the first to lay out regulations against content that endangers China's national security. Outlined in Article 10, the clause reads that no individual or unit may use the internet to engage in "criminal activities such as harming national security or disclosing secrets." This is significant, as previous legislation only vaguely touches upon the usage of the system's hardware without an explicit mention of national security. The fact that such language appeared in this document suggests that Beijing's understanding of the effects of the internet had become mature

---

[14] "Provisional Regulations Of The People's Republic Of China On The Management Of International Networking Of Computer Information Networks." Ministry of Commerce People's Republic of China. Ministry of Commerce People's Republic of China, February 1, 1996. http://english.mofcom.gov.cn/article/lawsdata/chinese-law/200211/20021100050748.shtml.

[15] "Laws of the People's Republic of China." AsianLII. AsianLII. Accessed January 29, 2022. http://www.asianlii.org/cn/legis/cen/laws/rfspocis719/.

[16] "Provisional Regulations Of The People's Republic Of China On The Management Of International Networking Of Computer Information Networks." Ministry of Commerce People's Republic of China. Ministry of Commerce People's Republic of China, February 1, 1996. http://english.mofcom.gov.cn/article/lawsdata/chinese-law/200211/20021100050748.shtml.

enough to appreciate the political implications of unregulated content within the national information sphere. Article 10 further lists the methods that may endanger China's national security, such as "to retrieve, replicate, create, or transmit information."[17]

Article 13 continues by touching on units "that provide computer information services domestically by using Internet information sources" and stipulates that they must be "inspected and approved by the regulations governing public telecom service providers."[18] This is a great contrast from the previous legislation as the text explicitly targets domestic internet users, requiring them to be approved by the state. It is also a reflection of the growing number of people using the internet within China's borders and the level of internet activity that is taking place among the Chinese population itself.

In December of 1997, the most comprehensive law regulating the internet came into effect, titled the Computer Information Network and Internet Security, Protection, and Management Regulations.[19] As defined in Article 1, this legislation builds upon the basis of previous documents. The most notable feature of this comprehensive legal text is its detailed definitions of the information that is forbidden and meant to be censored. This is clearly outlined in Articles 4 and 5. Specifically, information that incites to resist breaking the Constitution of the PRC, information that incites overthrow of the government or "socialist system," information that harms the unity of the nation, and information that injures the reputation of state organs.

Other than the above-mentioned details, the overall content of the legislation remains consistent with the overarching goals adhered to by previous provisional statements. As the U.S. Embassy in Beijing commented after the issuance of the 1997 regulation, "the new regulation contains no new prohibitions, and goes beyond the previous interim Internet regulation only in the level of detail on procedures, responsibilities, and penalties for violators."[20]

In fact, as noted by the embassy in the same document, even local internet service providers did not view the new regulation as posing any

---

[17] Ibid.

[18] Ibid.

[19] "Laws of the People's Republic of China." AsianLII. AsianLII. Accessed January 29, 2022. http://www.asianlii.org/cn/legis/cen/laws/rfspocis719/.

[20] "New PRC Internet Regulation." U.S. Embassy Beijing, January 1998. https://irp.fas.org/world/china/netreg.htm.

significant changes to their operations "since the new regulation contained no new restrictions." Even Deputy Secretary General of the State Council Steering Committee of National Information Infrastructure Yu Renlin said the U.S. Embassy, in the very same report, tried to suggest that "the new regulation was related to a relaxation of controls over Internet usage intended to encourage more widespread Internet use."

Through the series of revisions and the new issuance of regulations, a trend toward further clarity on information prohibition is evident. Language such as "national security," "state organs," and "unity of the nation" are explicitly named in the 1997 document. While the overall boundaries of content prohibited remain largely unchanged from 1994 through the end of the decade, the increasing clarity in language does seem to eliminate any ambiguity that might cause hindrances to widespread usage and activity in China's cyberspace.

The legacy of importing standards from the United States remains noteworthy, even as China develops its own technological ecosystem. The U.S. model of internet regulation fostered an environment that encouraged research and development. As regions like China's Greater Bay Area aspire to become the next global innovation hubs, the relationship between regulation and technology continues to evolve. This balance between openness and control, experimentation and censorship, has remained a defining characteristic of China's internet governance into the 21st century.

BIBLIOGRAPHY

Chandel, S., Z. Jingji, Y. Yunnan, S. Jingyao, and Z. Zhipeng. "The Golden Shield Project of China: A Decade Later—An in-Depth Study of the Great Firewall." In *2019 International Conference on Cyber-Enabled Distributed Computing and Knowledge Discovery (CyberC)*, 111–19. Guilin, China, 2019. https://doi.org/10.1109/CyberC.2019.00027.

Van Schaack, Beth. "China's Golden Shield: Is Cisco Systems Complicit?" Center for Internet and Society at Stanford Law School, March 24, 2015. https://cyberlaw.stanford.edu/blog/2015/03/china%E2%80%99s-golden-shield-cisco-systems-complicit.

Lai Stirland, Sarah. "Cisco Leak: 'Great Firewall' of China Was a Chance to Sell More Routers." WIRED, May 20, 2022. https://www.wired.com/2008/05/leaked-cisco-do/.

Lum, Thomas. "Internet Development and Information Control in the People's Republic of China." *CRS Report for Congress*, February 10, 2006. https://sgp. fas.org/crs/row/RL33167.pdf.

Zheng, H. "Regulating the Internet: China's Law and Practice." *Beijing Law Review* 4, no. 1 (2013): 37–41. https://doi.org/10.4236/blr.2013.41005.

Protocol

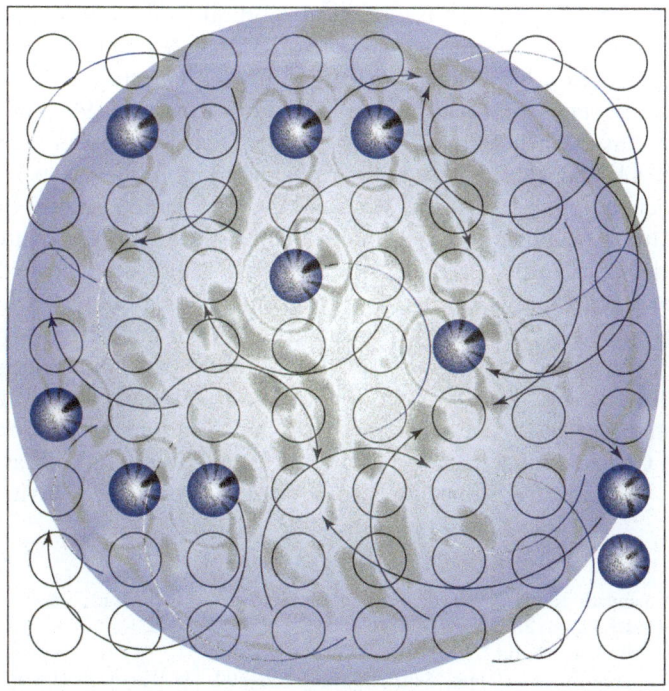

Internet #3 by Flora Weil

R. Shemakov, *Centralized*,
https://doi.org/10.1007/978-981-96-2937-4_8

Abstract This chapter examines the development of Russia's Information Security Doctrine as a response to the perception of threats in digital domains. Against the backdrop of Russia's invasion of Chechnya, the Doctrine articulated Russia's strategy for safeguarding its "information sphere"—a term encompassing cyber technology, media, and communication systems. It provided a framework for censoring media, surveilling online communication, and shaping public opinion through state-controlled information channels. Ultimately, the chapter underscores how cybersecurity was integrated into national security policies.

Keywords Cybernetics • Chechen war • Information security doctrine • Information warfare

Putin "was catapulted into the political spotlight" when he received 52 percent of the Russian presidential vote on March 26, 2000.[1] His success was predicated on his militaristic attitude toward Chechnya, a "de facto independent state" that had broken away from Russia in 1996 following the first Russo-Chechen war (1994–1996).[2] The war left an estimated 100,000 Chechens dead. This figure represented more than 10 percent of the Chechen population at that time and included large numbers of civilians.[3] After Chechnya declared independence, the fighting escalated. In 1999, the year Putin became Prime Minister, Russia was shocked by a series of terrorist attacks that the government attributed to Chechen forces. The first bombing took place at an apartment building in Moscow.

While the public was reeling from the first attack, a second bomb went off, followed by a third in Volfodonsk. The bombings resulted in 300 cumulative deaths. In the aftermath, Putin addressed the nation. He accused Chechen separatists of planting the bombs, a claim that was never proven. He declared that he "could not let terrorist activities go

---

[1] Rama Sampath Kumar, "President Putin: Good Czar or Bad Czar?," *Economic and Political Weekly* 35, no. 23 (June 3, 2000): 1904.

[2] Kumar, "President Putin," 1904.

[3] Senate Chairman Jesse Helms, "Senate Hearing 106–500. The War in Chechnya: Russia's Conduct, the Humanitarian Crisis, and United States Policy," § Committee on Foreign Relations (2000).

unpunished" and, in retaliation, he authorized a brutal assault on Chechnya.[4] The results of Putin's "relentless bombing raids" on Chechnya were catastrophic: thousands died; tens of thousands fled; and the Chechen capital, Grozny, was destroyed.[5] International media sources stood aghast at the extent of human suffering. But in Russia, where fear of Chechen rebels was omnipresent, Putin's decision bolstered his popularity at a crucial political moment leading into the presidential election.

Putin used television to reiterate his position as a defender of "Russian state interests," a stance that resonated in an anxious political climate.[6] Support from the media in relation to the Chechen crisis played an essential role in his electoral campaign. Putin represented the pro-Kremlin Unity Party, formed in September 1999. TV viewership and media consumption began to during this time. Throughout the election cycle, state television channels dedicated significantly more screen time to Unity than any other political coalition, including the competing Fatherland All-Russia Party (FAR). The year prior, in 1998, a financial crisis had sent Russia into financial freefall and the television broadcasting industry had been hit hard. The resulting "panic-driven interest in political and economic issues" that this caused among Russian citizens opened up a new market for TV producers.[7] News programs and talk shows "fill[ed] the air gaps."[8]

The presidential election represented the perfect topic for such channels. A series of investigative studies carried out after Putin's election noted the tendency of Unity voters to defer to state programs such as Russian Public Television (ORT) or Russian Radio and Television (RTR) as sources of information. Putin's presence dominated these channels: "The acting president [Putin] received about a third of the coverage that was given to all the candidates across all channels ... the state channels [were] heavily biased ... in the amount of coverage [Putin] received but

[4] Kumar, "President Putin," 1904.
[5] Kumar, "President Putin," 1904.
[6] White et al., "Media Effects," 197.
[7] Natalya A. Avseenko, "American Programs and Their Effectiveness on Russian Television," *American Studies International* 41, no. 1/2, Post Soviet American Studies International (February 2003): 204–5.
[8] Avseenko, "American Programs and Their Effectiveness," 205.

also in [their] deferential tone."[9] Commercial television "provided a more even-handed coverage" of candidates and parties, as later reported by the European Institute for the Media.[10] All the same, Russian voters cumulatively described state television as more reliable than other news sources, including commercial television.[11]

Individuals involved with ORT were directly involved in national political considerations. For instance, in 1997, Alexei K. Pushkov, then director of foreign affairs for ORT, also served on the Russian Council of Foreign and Defense Policies. (Prior to that, Pushkov had worked as a speechwriter for General Secretary Gorbachev.) Pushkov was outspoken in his criticism of NATO and asserted that NATO expansion would erode "mutual trust" between the United States and Russia.[12] His concerns foreshadowed conflicts that would bleed into the Putin era. Russia opposed the presence of nuclear weapons or NATO military forces on "territories of future member states" and "new East European member states."[13] Pushkov also raised the issue of the Baltic states, including Ukraine, with regard to NATO membership. If these states became NATO members, he warned, it would "spark a serious crisis in relations between Russia and the West."[14] "Such a move [was] clearly unacceptable" to the Kremlin.[15] The United States promised that these events would not occur. But Pushkov, speaking for Russia's interests, dismissed these "high-sounding promises" and called for a formal agreement to codify the extent of NATO's reach.[16]

In 1997, Russian President Boris Yeltsin and U.S. President Bill Clinton were engaged in frequent communications on the subject of NATO. On April 15, Yeltsin petitioned Clinton to offer him a guarantee that NATO

[9] Stephen White, Sarah Oates, and Ian McAllister, "Media Effects and Russian Elections, 1999–2000," *British Journal of Political Science* 35, no. 2 (April 2005): 197.

[10] White et al., "Media Effects," 191.

[11] This bias was, as expected, more prevalent among Unity voters. White et al., "Media Effects," 200.

[12] Alexei K. Pushkov, "Don't Isolate Us: A Russian View of NATO Expansion," *The National Interest*, no. 47 (Spring 1997): 59.

[13] Pushkov, "Don't Isolate Us," 59.

[14] Pushkov, "Don't Isolate Us," 59.

[15] Pushkov, "Don't Isolate Us," 59.

[16] Pushkov, "Don't Isolate Us," 59.

would not "embrace the former Soviet republics ... especially Ukraine."[17] Yeltsin indicated his concern and disapproval of U.S./Ukrainian relations, which he equated with "pressure tactics."[18] He also took issue with U.S. naval activity around Crimea. Yeltsin proposed a private "gentleman's agreement" between himself and Clinton, a verbal deal that could be kept off-the-record.[19] Yeltsin would "accept" that Russia "[had] no claims on other countries" in return for Clinton's word that NATO would exclude the "former Soviet Union."[20]

Yeltsin concluded his argument with an ultimatum. He reminded Clinton that if NATO were to accept "even one" former Soviet Republic, the Russian Duma would reject a NATO-Russian charter.[21] Clinton responded with a polite but firm dismissal. He stated that he could not make an off-the-record deal to that effect and that Yeltsin's proposed agreement would "undermine the whole spirit of NATO."[22] The pair ended the conversation and agreed to maintain an open line of communication.

Yeltsin and Clinton spoke again in 1999 on the subject of Vladimir Putin. In a telephone memorandum dated September 8, both parties expressed concern about the state of the U.S./Russian relationship. Yeltsin spoke first about the upcoming Russian election. He shared his choice of Putin as a potential successor whom he was "very much convinced [would] be supported as a candidate."[23] Yeltsin promised that he would be a "highly qualified partner" on the international stage.[24] But Yeltsin knew that Putin, and the United States, would have to deal with conflict in

[17] Bill Clinton and Boris Yeltsin, "Declassified Documents Concerning Russian President Boris Yeltsin: Memorandum of Conversation. Morning Meeting with Russian President Yeltsin: NATO-Russia, START, ABM/TMD. Declassified March 21, 2017." (William J. Clinton Presidential Library & Museum, March 21, 1997).

[18] Clinton and Yeltsin, "Morning Meeting with Russian President Yeltsin," March, 1997.

[19] Clinton and Yeltsin, "Morning Meeting with Russian President Yeltsin," March, 1997.

[20] Clinton and Yeltsin, "Morning Meeting with Russian President Yeltsin," March, 1997.

[21] Clinton and Yeltsin, "Morning Meeting with Russian President Yeltsin," March, 1997.

[22] Clinton and Yeltsin, "Morning Meeting with Russian President Yeltsin," March, 1997.

[23] Bill Clinton and Boris Yeltsin, "Declassified Documents Concerning Russian President Boris Yeltsin: Memorandum of Telephone Conversation. Telephone Conversation with Russian President Yeltsin. Declassified November 19, 2009." (William J. Clinton Presidential Library & Museum, September 8, 1999).

[24] Clinton and Yeltsin, "Telephone Conversation with Russian President Yeltsin," September, 1999.

Chechnya and Dagestan. The Russian president was adamant that this region constituted an "international center of terrorism."[25] Russia was prepared to "give them a very strong rebuffing," and Yeltsin requested Clinton's support, "morally" as well as "politically."[26] Clinton indicated his full support for any counterterrorism measure, but he cautioned Russia to consider the risks posed to civilians "caught in the crossfire."[27]

Several months later, in a meeting between Clinton, Yeltsin, and a group of American and Russian diplomats, it was evident that tensions had risen. Here, the congenial tone of the presidents' previous conversations vanished. After a series of terse greetings, Yeltsin said, "I know we are not upset at each other. We were just throwing some jabs."[28] The presidents sparred over the ABM Treaty. At last, Yeltsin stated, "Just give Europe to Russia." Russia was "half Europe," but the United States had no reason to care about European affairs.[29] Clinton scoffed at this. "[Will] you want Asia too?" The tense conversation circled back to the topic of the election, with Yeltsin assuring Clinton that Putin was bound to become the next Russian president. Indeed, Yeltsin's final words seemed to anticipate the accusations of electoral corruption that the United States levied against Putin in the wake of his victory: "I will do everything possible for him to win — legally, of course."[30] The United States later criticized the Russian media as one factor in an electoral campaign tinged with corruption.

In May, following his inauguration, Putin moved at once to consolidate power in the presidency. He called for a referendum to revise the Russian Constitution of 1993 and extend the presidential term from four to seven years. A publication from June of 2000 expressed concern that "if this should materialize ... Putin could stay in power till 2011."[31] Putin

[25] Clinton and Yeltsin, "Telephone Conversation with Russian President Yeltsin," September, 1999.

[26] Clinton and Yeltsin, "Telephone Conversation with Russian President Yeltsin," September, 1999.

[27] Clinton and Yeltsin, "Telephone Conversation with Russian President Yeltsin," September, 1999.

[28] Bill Clinton and Boris Yeltsin, "Declassified Documents Concerning Russian President Boris Yeltsin: Memorandum of Conversation. Meeting with Russian President Yeltsin. Declassified December 11, 2009." (William J. Clinton Presidential Library & Museum, November 19, 1999).

[29] Clinton and Yeltsin, "Meeting with Russian President Yeltsin," November, 1999.

[30] Clinton and Yeltsin, "Meeting with Russian President Yeltsin," November, 1999.

[31] Putin served as president from 2000 to 2008 and then resumed his position in 2012, far surpassing the seven-year benchmark in total years in office. Kumar, "President Putin," 1904.

publicized his support of the Russian intelligence services (he had served as head of the FSB under Yeltsin in 1998). As president, he pushed for this organization to control the Russian media with the express purpose of preventing dissent over the crisis in Chechnya from reaching the public.[32] Putin recognized the power of the collective media and dedicated himself to crafting a distinct narrative for Russia's present and its future.[33]

He stressed a need to "[return] the glory of the Soviet Union on the national level" and to expand Russian control into nearby territories.[34] But Putin feared that the West, particularly the United States, would threaten the success of these missions. He believed that Western influence would corrupt the Russian way of life through the spread of "unacceptable ideas, norms, practices, and behaviors."[35] The rise of the internet as a vehicle for Western ideology was an immediate and vital concern. Putin sought to turn this force back against the West through targeted propaganda and the introduction of censorship laws that strangled oppositional expression.

Putin's Information Security Doctrine of the Russian Federation, enacted in 2000, addressed the fear of foreign interference in Russian affairs by giving the president sweeping power over the so-called information sphere, a term used to encompass both cyber technology and the human interactions shaped by that technology.[36] The official purpose of the Doctrine was to protect Russia's military and security-related information, but neither category was well defined. It was unclear how much legislative power the state gained when Putin signed the Doctrine into law. The Russian public, particularly the press, noted that the Doctrine dedicated a "disproportionate amount of attention" to the media.[37] This was because the commercial media and the internet were areas in which the Kremlin had not yet assured its control over the spread of information.

---

[32] Kumar, "President Putin," 1904.

[33] On the evening of his election, Putin "openly acknowledged that there had not been equal access to the media by all candidates" and promised to "respond to the tens of millions of Russian voters who were expressing their dissatisfaction," including the "protest voters" who supported his campaign. "Senate Hearing 106–702. Hearing Before the Subcommittee on European Affairs of the Committee on Foreign Relations United States Senate," § One Hundred Sixth Congress (April 12 2000).

[34] Media Ajir and Bethany Vailliant, "Russian Information Warfare: Implications for Deterrence Theory," *Strategic Studies Quarterly* 12, no. 3 (Fall 2018): 70–71.

[35] Ajir and Vailliant, "Russian Information Warfare," 70–71.

[36] Ajir and Vailliant, "Russian Information Warfare," 74.

[37] Carmen, "Translation and Analysis of the Doctrine of Information Security," 344–6.

The Information Security Doctrine addressed Putin's concerns by adapting Soviet-esque censorship techniques to the modern digital era. Putin wanted to avoid the pitfalls of Soviet-era policies. He recognized that overt forms of restriction, such as "the criminalization of dissent or the censorship of ideologically unacceptable ideas," would only encourage "subversion" and garner international disapproval.[38] Thus, he focused on shaping "genuine consensus" among the public by blacklisting opposition publications while empowering state institutions to regulate and publish information.[39]

The Information Security Doctrine was divided into three segments: "Information Security of the Russian Federation," "Methods for Ensuring the Information Security of the Russian Federation," and "The Main Propositions of the Russian State Information Security Policy and Urgent Measures to Realize it."[40] The first section described the state's objective to adhere to the provisions of the Russian Constitution—including "freedom of mass information and the prohibition of censorship"—while also ensuring the "unconditional maintenance of law and order."[41] Putin granted the state a critical role in this process by promising to expand state media resources and to increase communication security. The Doctrine showed how Putin's stance on state media differed from his approach to citizen or public media use. Citizens were expected to view the "information sphere" as a limited privilege.[42] For instance, Putin acknowledged the "contradictions" created by the rise of digital "free exchange" and the need to preserve "limitations" on communications, including those through new social networks.[43] Citizens were thus the recipients of state information that they were not invited to question or counter. In contrast, the state media was responsible for *producing* information to shape, and reshape, public opinion in accordance with the president's needs.

The second section of the Information Security Doctrine delineated a path toward a more secure Russian Federation. Necessary steps included

---

[38] Doughlas Carmen, trans., "Translation and Analysis of the Doctrine of Information Security of the Russian Federation: Mass Media and the Politics of Identity," Pacific Rim Law & Policy Journal Association 11, no. 2 (2002), 341.

[39] Carmen, "Translation and Analysis of the Doctrine of Information Security," 341.

[40] "Information Security Doctrine of The Russian Federation, Approved by President of the Russian Federation Vladimir Putin on September 9, 2000," September 9, 2000.

[41] "Information Security Doctrine," 2.

[42] "Information Security Doctrine," 9.

[43] "Information Security Doctrine," 8–9.

producing legislation to "concretiz[e] the legal norms establishing responsibility for law violations in … information security" and vesting that power in the hands of state officials.[44] The Doctrine affirmed the president's intention to revise national legislation in order to tighten security. It noted a plan to increase the "law enforcement activities of … executive bodies" so violators of the law could be brought "to justice."[45] Several pages of the Doctrine addressed the possibility of a threat to the Russian economy through a breach of the information sphere. This segment recalled Soviet-era debates regarding benefits and risks generated by the use of computer technology for economic purposes. The Doctrine affirmed that a nationalized security system with a tight regulatory framework would best safeguard the economy.

A persistent trend throughout the Information Security Doctrine was the notion that the West might gain power over Russia through the information sphere. Therefore, the Doctrine foregrounded the importance of "countering the monopolization of … information infrastructure," or the predominance of Western influence over the Russian internet.[46] The Doctrine argued that Western propaganda was bound to filter into Russia; the state had to respond with "counterpropaganda activities" to prevent the spread of "disinformation about Russian domestic policy."[47] In 1997, the U.S. Pentagon obtained a draft of Russia's internet security legislation. A report published by *Inside the Pentagon* noted a sudden and dramatic rise in Russian concerns about "cyber attacks … information warfare … computer viruses," and the like.[48] The author, Holly Porteuous, cited the opinion of Mary Fitzgerald, a Russian military security expert. Fitzgerald noted that Russia had been building toward a systematic plan for "information warfare" since the 1980s, but, in the modern day, "Russian military literature" credited the information sphere as "having an impact on par with weapons of mass destruction."[49]

---

[44] "Information Security Doctrine," 10–11.

[45] "Information Security Doctrine," 12.

[46] "Information Security Doctrine," 15.

[47] "Information Security Doctrine," 15.

[48] Holly Porteous, "Russians Express Angst on Information Warfare in New Security Doctrine," *Inside the Pentagon* 13, no. 41 (October 9, 1997): 1.

[49] Porteous, "Russians Express Angst," 16. Around this time, in 1998, the United States Senate held a hearing to discuss the fear of a cyber attack. The Director of Central Intelligence stated at this time that "Russia and China, [had] government-sponsored information warfare programs with both offensive and defense applications" that might be turned against "a

The majority of the Doctrine consisted of offensive policies that Putin framed as defensive policies. The evidently self-protective document legislated a significant increase in the power of the state. It authorized heightened security forces in response to situations with little apparent political import. For instance, in a section on "emergency conditions," the Information Security Doctrine described the risks associated with the potential "unsanctioned access" of individuals to information operating services in the event of a national crisis.[50] These risks included: endangering the lives of citizens, causing unnecessary panic, and inspiring "psychic stress" among the public through the spread of falsities.[51] To mitigate this concern, the Doctrine suggested the introduction of new programs that would protect information systems related to important organizations and enterprises.

Russia's degree of concern over the spread of information and misinformation was evident in the final legislation of the Information Security Doctrine that authorized Russia to take active steps toward refuting the content of Western media communications" or to block such communications from reaching the public. Putin justified this approach with allegations about the supposed inaccuracy of Western publications. But the Information Security Doctrine reinforced the viability of state "narrative manipulation ... framing ... agenda-setting."[52] It further implied to the Russian public that any Western information was suspect.

Putin's role in developing the Information Security Doctrine should not be understated. This document, like other national security legislation, was authored by the Russian Security Council, an organization that included Putin and upon which he exerted tremendous influence. The Council had formed in 1992. The 1993 Russian Constitution established "the Russian President [as] the single most important person amongst [its] permanent members," a group that included the Prime Minister, Ministers of Foreign Affairs and Defense, the Director of the Federal

---

stronger military power such as the U.S." This hearing was followed in 1999 by the United States Government Information Security Act. "Government Information Security Act of 1999, to Accompany S. 1993 To Reform Government Information Security by Strengthening Information Security Practices Throughout the Federal Government," Senate Report (Washington, D.C.: One Hundred Sixth Congress, April 10, 2000).

[50] "Information Security Doctrine," 24.

[51] "Information Security Doctrine," 24.

[52] Kerr, "The Russian Model of Internet Control," 6.

Security Bureau, and the Security Council Secretary.[53] Putin served on the council as Prime Minister in 1999. His power increased as president once he could control the work of the council at multiple points in the legislative process. For instance, Putin might introduce ideas to the council as a member, use his status to push for their inclusion in legislation drafts, and himself sign those drafts into law. Putin's role in this system suggests that the Information Security Doctrine addressed his personal security concerns.

The Information Security Doctrine is further contextualized by a series of revisions to Russia's military and security policies in 1999 and 2000. In 1999, the Russian Security Council, including Putin, authored an updated "national security concept" and "military doctrine."[54] These documents were approved shortly before Putin's election. The new military doctrine addressed the apparent limitations of a previous version introduced in 1993. It expanded the focus of Russian security concerns from the national to the international level, highlighting the rise of NATO and the dominance of the United States within that organization.

The new security doctrine focused on the situation in Chechnya as a primary concern. It defined Russian intervention in Chechnya as "counter-terrorism," making it possible for Russia to take action against Chechnya under the terms of the 1994 Russian Federation Criminal Code which distinguished terrorism as a crime.[55] The National Security Concept and Military Doctrine affirmed in 2000 that Moscow "considered international terrorism a major threat."[56] The Information Security Doctrine, while not expressly militaristic, was another facet of Putin's push for heightened security and it responded to the same concerns raised in the National Security Concept and Military Doctrine. These included "new sources of threat" toward Russia such as Western influence, the spread of anti-Kremlin narratives—termed "extremism"—and other "soft security" risks.[57]

Putin believed that the United States disapproved of his presidency, and he was correct in this respect. In fact, an unsettled U.S. Congress convened just before the 2000 election to discuss the matter. One speaker at

[53] Amina Afzal, "Russian Security Policy," *Strategic Studies* 25, no. 1 (Spring 2005): 68.
[54] Afzal, "Russian Security Policy," 69.
[55] Afzal, "Russian Security Policy," 73.
[56] Afzal, "Russian Security Policy," 73.
[57] Afzal, "Russian Security Policy," 69–77.

this meeting was a William Green, a Naval Reserves Intelligence Officer and college professor. Green said of Putin, "He is in many ways an unattractive character given his KGB background ... Putin's tactic of tying renewed war in Chechnya to his national leadership has attracted much criticism [but] ... at home it may very well be the factor that propels him to the presidency."[58] In saying this, Green reiterated the role of media coverage in Putin's Russia. Dr. Peter Pry, a former CIA analyst, also addressed Congress. Pry criticized the Russian electoral process, saying that Russia had made a mockery of "free and fair elections."[59] Worse still was the climate of heightened tension between Russia and the United States, including military and even nuclear threats from the Russian side. Green concurred with Pry's assessment, referencing the recent changes to Russia's National Security Doctrine and Military Doctrine. The new Security Doctrine contained "much looser terms for describing the conditions under which nuclear weapons might be used," in contrast to a 1997 version which spoke of "nuclear deterrence."[60] Green blamed the United States for "reckless behavior" and a failure to acknowledge or respond to the simmering conflict with Russia.[61]

The United States' criticism of Putin rose in response to the situation in Chechnya. An article published in the *New York Times* in March of 2000 contrasted Putin's approach to Chechnya with that of Boris Yeltsin. While president, Yeltsin had failed to align the state and the military due to his desire to compromise with the West on political matters. Putin, however, "explicitly renounced" Yeltsin's 1996 pact with Chechen rebel leaders, claiming that this step was in the interests of the Chechen citizenry: "The Chechens ... are not a defeated people. They are a liberated people."[62] The *New York Times* article condemned Putin's actions. It accused the Russian army of "all out assaults ... with no discrimination between civilians and fighters," including "torture, beatings, rapes, and killings in prison camps."[63] With these horrors brought to light, the article

---

[58] William Green, "House Hearing Before the Committee on Government Reform," § One Hundred Sixth Congress (January 24, 2000).

[59] Dr. Peter Pry, "House Hearing Before the Committee on Government Reform," § One Hundred Sixth Congress (January 24, 2000).

[60] Green, "House Hearing."

[61] Green, "House Hearing."

[62] John Lloyd, "The Logic of Vladimir Putin," *The New York Times Magazine*, March 19, 2000.

[63] Lloyd, "The Logic of Vladimir Putin."

spoke to overarching differences between the Western and Russian perspectives. It said that West saw "the K.G.B. as an undifferentiated horror" and that "the people who care most about democracy in Russia do fear [Putin] ... and say they have cause."[64] However, the author was forced to acknowledge the admiration most of the Russian public had for Putin's leadership. The same month that this article reached the press, the United States Senate Committee on Foreign Relations convened to discuss "the humanitarian crisis" in Chechnya and how the United States should respond.[65]

On March 1, Senate Chairman Jesse Helms used fervent language as he described the Chechen conflict. In the first minutes of the meeting, he called Russian behavior "reprehensible," spoke out against the "atrocities" and "brutality" of the war, and added that "the enormous human suffering caused by Russia's brutal campaign [is something] the world seems perfectly content to ignore."[66] Helms implied that the United States would have to be the nation to lead the charge against Putin. The Chairman also addressed the role of the media, both Western and Russian, in the perpetuation of Russia's military actions. He spoke to the importance of objective news reports in the face of Western denial of the war. Putin contributed to this situation, the Chairman claimed, because he had carried out "systematic repression of the press," ranging from propaganda campaigns to the detainment of journalists.[67]

In one high-profile case, Andrei Babitsky, a journalist for Radio Free Europe/Radio Liberty who published accurate but critical accounts about Russia's military, vanished after he was detained by Russian officials. The United States Senate "unanimously condemn[ed]" Babitsky's treatment through Resolution 261, passed shortly before the March 1 meeting.[68] Resolution 262 followed, also with a unanimous vote, upholding the right of the Chechen people to defend themselves against Russian forces. Resolution 262 further requested that Russia allow international agencies for human aid into Chechnya and that the Russian government investigate charges raised against Russian soldiers to their full extent. The day after

[64] Lloyd, "The Logic of Vladimir Putin."
[65] Chairman Helms, "Senate Hearing 106–500. The War in Chechnya."
[66] Chairman Helms, "Senate Hearing 106–500. The War in Chechnya."
[67] Chairman Helms, "Senate Hearing 106–500. The War in Chechnya."
[68] Chairman Helms, "Senate Hearing 106–500. The War in Chechnya."

these two resolutions were passed, Babitsky was "found" by the Kremlin and returned to his family.[69] Nonetheless, the case illustrated the reach of the state and the risks journalists undertook when they spoke out against Putin's regime.

Thomas Dine, president of the Radio Free Europe/Radio Liberty program, spoke at the Senate meeting with respect to the Babitsky case. "Media freedom is the basis of all other freedoms," he said.[70] But Russia's treatment of Babitsky was just one facet of a general slide toward Soviet-era authoritarianism under Putin. The Senate feared that Russia would prevent its own citizens from learning the truth about the conflict in Chechnya and cover up accounts of abuses of power on Putin's part. In response to Putin's repeated claims that he was liberating Chechnya from terrorism, the Senate stated: "What is being done … is not a liberation struggle … It is not an acceptable or understandable response to domestic terrorism … It is abhorrent."[71] It was clear that Russia and the United States stood in opposition to one another, and debates over suppression of the media in Russia intersected with United States' concerns over human rights violations under Putin.

Without a doubt, the United States observed and sought to combat Putin's early efforts to violate the principles of democracy and to stifle the spread of public opinion. And knowing that the United States believed that "America's most effective tool in promoting … democracy is the example of the United States itself." Therefore, the expressed intent to expand internet access into Russia meant encouraging "the dissemination of materials on democracy," and the support of "any program that increases the flow in information" within Russia.[72] But these ventures were difficult to undertake in the political climate created by the Information Security

---

[69] Chairman Helms, "Senate Hearing 106–500. The War in Chechnya." Babitsky was forced into a Russian filtration camp following his detainment on January 16th, 2000. Russia had multiple camps stationed in Chechnya, with the one where Babitsky was placed notable for the "horrors" prisoners endured there. The FSB and the Russian Ministry of the Interior (MVD) both had a hand in the operation of these institutions.

[70] Thomas Dine, "The War in Chechnya: Russia's Conduct, the Humanitarian Crisis, and United States Policy," United States Senate Committee on Foreign Relations (2000).

[71] Minnesota Senator Russel D. Feingold, "Senate Hearing 106–500. The War in Chechnya: Russia's Conduct, the Humanitarian Crisis, and United States Policy," § Committee on Foreign Relations (2000).

[72] "Senate Hearing 106–702. Hearing Before the Subcommittee on European Affairs."

Doctrine that renounced such actions on the part of foreign nations. For instance, under the terms of the Doctrine, the United States Senate Resolutions 261 and 262 would have constituted "external threats ... in the defense sphere"; any information published from the perspective of the United States would fall under the umbrella of "subversive and sabotage activities ... carried out by methods of informational and psychological influence."[73] The Doctrine licensed Russia to respond with intelligence operations and by integrating information security more fully into the "defense sphere."[74] Putin designated these measures as protective. But the terms of the Doctrine gave Putin and the Russian Security Service the power to silence public commentary or debate any matter of national importance by declaring it a security threat.

The third and final section of the Doctrine affirmed that future "provision of information to the public" was henceforth contingent upon "the restrictions established by the legislation of the Russian Federation."[75] Furthermore, it impressed upon the public the necessity of federal programs designed to monitor the spread of information and noted the necessity of legislative measures to support these projects. This section of the Information Security Doctrine contained several key points related to the distribution of security powers within the Russian Federation. It asserted that the president controlled global national security policies as well as those in the information domain. It encouraged the Security Council (including the president, Putin) to continue seeking out and identifying security threats. Finally, it authorized "federal executive bodies" and "interagency and state commissions" to enact the terms of the Doctrine with the full support of the Council.[76]

Why is the Information Security Doctrine significant among Putin's myriad political and legislative actions during his first year in office? In this document, Putin moved beyond the censorship and propaganda techniques that won him the presidency. He tapped into the ever-expanding cyber domain and established the internet and the media as two areas central to consolidating power. Far from being a technical document, the

---

[73] "Information Security Doctrine," 22.
[74] "Information Security Doctrine," 23.
[75] "Information Security Doctrine," 26.
[76] "Information Security Doctrine," 31.

Information Security Doctrine served as a blueprint for Russia's 21st-century authoritarianism—one centered not on tanks or territory, but on controlling the invisible flows of information.

BIBLIOGRAPHY

Kumar, Rama Sampath. "President Putin: Good Czar or Bad Czar?" *Economic and Political Weekly* 35, no. 23 (June 3, 2000): 1904.

Helms, Jesse. "Senate Hearing 106–500. The War in Chechnya: Russia's Conduct, the Humanitarian Crisis, and United States Policy." Committee on Foreign Relations, 2000.

Avseenko, Natalya A. "American Programs and Their Effectiveness on Russian Television." *American Studies International* 41, no. 1/2 (February 2003): 204–5.

White, Stephen, Sarah Oates, and Ian McAllister. "Media Effects and Russian Elections, 1999–2000." *British Journal of Political Science* 35, no. 2 (April 2005): 197.

Pushkov, Alexei K. "Don't Isolate Us: A Russian View of NATO Expansion." *The National Interest*, no. 47 (Spring 1997): 59.

Clinton, Bill, and Boris Yeltsin. "Declassified Documents Concerning Russian President Boris Yeltsin: Memorandum of Conversation. Morning Meeting with Russian President Yeltsin: NATO-Russia, START, ABM/TMD. Declassified March 21, 2017." William J. Clinton Presidential Library & Museum, March 21, 1997.

Ajir, Media, and Bethany Vailliant. "Russian Information Warfare: Implications for Deterrence Theory." *Strategic Studies Quarterly* 12, no. 3 (Fall 2018): 70–71.

Carmen, Douglas, trans. "Translation and Analysis of the Doctrine of Information Security of The Russian Federation: Mass Media and the Politics of Identity." *Pacific Rim Law & Policy Journal Association* 11, no. 2 (2002). 341.

"Information Security Doctrine of the Russian Federation, Approved by President of the Russian Federation Vladimir Putin on September 9, 2000." September 9, 2000.

Porteous, Holly. "Russians Express Angst on Information Warfare in New Security Doctrine." *Inside the Pentagon* 13, no. 41 (October 9, 1997): 1.

Afzal, Amina. "Russian Security Policy." *Strategic Studies* 25, no. 1 (Spring 2005): 68.

Green, William. "House Hearing Before the Committee on Government Reform." One Hundred Sixth Congress, January 24, 2000.

Pry, Peter. "House Hearing Before the Committee on Government Reform." One Hundred Sixth Congress, January 24, 2000.

Lloyd, John. "The Logic of Vladimir Putin." *The New York Times Magazine*, March 19, 2000.

Dine, Thomas. "The War in Chechnya: Russia's Conduct, the Humanitarian Crisis, and United States Policy." United States Senate Committee on Foreign Relations, 2000.

Feingold, Russel D. "Senate Hearing 106–500. The War in Chechnya: Russia's Conduct, the Humanitarian Crisis, and United States Policy." Committee on Foreign Relations, 2000.

The manufacturer's authorised representative in the EU is Springer
Nature Customer Service Centre GmbH, Europaplatz 3, 69115 Heidelberg,
Germany. If you have any concerns regarding our products, please
contact ProductSafety@springernature.com

Printed and bound by CPI Group (UK) Ltd, Croydon, CR0 4YY
27/04/2026
02097570-0006